# WORKING WOMEN

*Issues and Challenges*

# WORKING WOMEN
## *Issues and Challenges*

*Dr. Rameshwari Pandya*
*Ms. Dhara Thakkar*

MADHAV BOOKS
GURGAON (HARYANA)

First Published – 2010

ISBN: 978-81-907891-5-8



*Published by*

**MADHAV BOOKS**
F-2562, Palam Vihar
Gurgaon-122 017 (Haryana)
Phone : 0124-2365193, 9810373248

# CONTENTS

# PREFACE

A woman is the mother of the race and liaison between generations. From times immemorial, woman along with man has formed an integral part of the social structure throughout the world. Consistent with the long-term trend the presence of women in work force continues to increase. The employment of women has opened up new vistas for women; shifting interest from household duties to work outside. The features like low pay, non-recognition and invisibilization of work often characterize women paid work. The crux of the problem of women's employment lies in the dilemma of her dual responsibilities in being a housewife, a mother as well as an employee and a producer of income for her family. Hence, the problem is not with the women as officer or at any other post, but the very attitude of men and sometimes of women themselves, which cannot be changed, is the problem. Thus, in addition, the physical and psychological stress at job, together affect women employees health, morale and commitment adversely. As the problem of violence against women is multifaceted, the NCW has adopted a multi-pronged strategy to tackle the problem. The Commission has initiated generation of legal awareness among women, thus equipping them with the knowledge of their legal rights and with a capacity to use these rights. It assists women in redressal of their grievances through pre-litigation services. A research was conducted with the objectives to study the problems faced by working women of Baroda, to find out the overall, job related and household work related problems of working women in relation to their Age, Type of family, Experience and Distance from the home to their workplace. To study the problems of working women 120 working women of Baroda city of Gujarat State were selected. The Structured Questionnaire for collecting the information for the study of Problems of working women of Baroda in the year 2008-09 was constructed from various books, journals, and papers, personal experience of the investigation and also through discussion with experts. It is to be remembered that majority of the respondents were from younger age group, belonged to nuclear family and Hindu Religion. If we are serious about substantially improving the economic status of working women of the economy, we have to device coping up strategies which can help to improve their working environment and to manage their stress.

# 1

# INTRODUCTION

## WOMEN

A woman is the mother of the race and liaison between generations. It is the mother who have sustained the growth of the society and moulded the future of the nation. In the emerging complex social scenario, women have a pivotal role to play. They can no longer be considered as mere harbingers of peace, but they are emerging as a source of power and a symbol of progress. Their work is imminent individually, in family, in society, in nation and in the economy on the whole. From times immemorial, woman along with man has formed an integral part of the social structure throughout the world. In Indian society, she has played important and continuous role. Variation in the status of woman according to the cultural milieu, family structure, case, class and proprietary rights etc. have been taking place from time to time. Her role in various walks of life has greatly contributed to the evolution of values, which lead to all round progress of society at large.

The majority of women are burdened with dual gaps of gender bias and resource deprivation. Women in these ways, have a lot of balancing to do between home and workplace, including balancing between social and personal requirements. The issues of maternity, menopause, parenthood, gender roles, conditions at home and workplace, familiar and social support at all, often blight women's lives in the long run. Modern women have the dual responsibilities of concentrating on the family as well as at work. Married women hold greater responsibility within the family when compared with the unmarried ones. Working women form a major chunck of society. So, the problems of the working women are multifarious and multidimensional. Therefore, their presence, aspiration and problems cannot be ignored.

## WOMEN EMPLOYMENT IN INDIA

India's economy has undergone a substantial transformation since the country's independence in 1947. Agriculture now accounts for only one-third of the gross domestic product (GDP), down from 59 percent in 1950, and a wide range of modern industries and support services now exist. In spite of these changes, agriculture continues to dominate employment, employing two-thirds of all workers. India faced economic problems in the late 1980s and early 1990s that were exacerbated by the Persian Gulf Crisis. Starting in 1992, India began to implement trade liberalization measures. But the results of unfettered operation of market forces are not always equitable, especially in India, where some groups are likely to be subjected to disadvantage as a result of globalization. Women constitute one such vulnerable group.

Since the times immemorial, worth of the work done or services rendered by women has not been recognized. India is a multifaceted society where no generalization could apply to the entire nation's various regional, religious, social, and economic groups. Nevertheless, certain broad circumstances in which Indian women live affect the ways they participate in the economy. Indian society is extremely hierarchical with virtually everyone ranked relative to others according to their caste (or caste-like group), class, wealth, and power. This ranking even exists in areas where it is not openly acknowledged, such as certain business settings. Though specific customs vary from region to region within the country, there are different standards of behaviour for men and women that carry over into the work environment. Women are expected to be chaste and especially modest in all actions that may constrain their ability to perform in the workplace on an equal basis with men. Another related aspect of life in India is that women are generally confined to home thus restricting their mobility and face seclusion. The women face constraints beyond those already placed on them by other hierarchical practices. These cultural rules place some Indian women, particularly those of lower caste, in a paradoxical situation: when a family suffers economically, people often think that a woman should go out and work, yet at the same time the woman's participation in employment outside the home is viewed as "slightly inappropriate, subtly wrong, and definitely dangerous to their chastity and womanly virtue". When a family recovers from an economic crisis or attempts to improve its status, women may be kept at home as a demonstration of the family's morality and as a symbol of its financial security.

A section of Indian women-the elite and the upper middle class- have gained by the exposure to the global network. More women are engaged in business enterprises, in international platforms like the Inter-Parliamentary Union, and have greater career opportunities as a result of international network. Freer movement of goods and capital is helpful to this section. But most women continue to remain marginalized as they are generally employed in a chain of work and seldom allowed independent charge of her job. Sharing of responsibility at workplace or taking independent decisions is still a remote possibility for them. Economic independence of women is important as it enhances their ability to take decisions and exercise freedom of choice, action. Many of the working women, who control their own income, do contribute towards the economic needs of family as and when required. They often participate in discussions at their work place and their views are given due weightage before any final decision.

Working women do use and spend their income at their own will but sometimes permission of the husband becomes necessary for the purpose. However when it comes to making investments, they often leave it to their husbands or other male members of the family to invest on their behalf. Many of them do not take decision even in case of important investments, like, life insurance, national saving schemes or other tax saving investments. Working women do feel concerned about the economic needs of the family but when not consulted in such matters, they regret being ignored especially when they contribute monetarily towards economic well being of the family.

After globalization, women are able to get more jobs but the work they get is more casual in nature or is the one that men do not prefer to do or is left by them to move to higher or better jobs. Globalization has indeed raised hopes of women for a better and elevated status arising out of increased chances to work but, at the same time, it has put them in a highly contradictory situation where they have the label of economically independent paid workers but are not able to enjoy their economic liberty in real sense of the term. India is the first among countries to give women equal franchise and has a highly credible record with regard to the enactment of laws to protect and promote the interests of women, but women continue to be denied economic, social and legal rights and privileges. Though they are considered to be equal partners in progress, yet they remain subjected to repression, marginalization and exploitation.

It has been advocated by many researchers that independent earning opportunities reduce the economic dependence of woman on man and increase her bargaining power in the family. This bargaining power depends on the nature of work she is employed in. But the income earning activities increase the workload of a woman unless the man accepts an increased share in domestic work. Since globalization is introducing technological inputs, women are being marginalized in economic activities, men traditionally being offered new scopes of learning and training. Consequently, female workers are joining the informal sector or casual labor force more than ever before. For instance, while new rice technology has given rise to higher use of female labour, the increased work-load for women is in operations that are unrecorded, and often unpaid, since these fall within the category of home production activities. The weaker sections, especially the women, are denied the physical care they deserve. There is, thus, hardly any ability for the majority of Indian women to do valuable functioning; the "capability" to choose from alternatives is conspicuous by absence.

Although most women in India work and contribute to the economy in one form or another, much of their work is not documented or accounted for official statistics. Women plow fields and harvest crops while working on farms, women weave and make handicrafts while working in household industries, women sell food and gather wood while working in the informal sector. Additionally, women are traditionally responsible for the daily household chores (e.g., cooking, fetching water, and looking after children). Although the cultural restrictions women face are changing, women are still not as free as men to participate in the formal economy. In the past, cultural restrictions were the primary impediments to female employment now however; the shortage of jobs throughout the country contributes to low female employment as well. The Indian census divides workers into two categories: "main" and "marginal" workers. Main workers include people who worked for 6 months or more during the year, while marginal workers include those who worked for a shorter period. Many of these workers are agricultural labourers. Unpaid farm and family enterprise workers are supposed to be included in either the main worker or marginal worker category, as appropriate. Women account for a small proportion of the formal Indian labour force, even though the number of female main workers has grown faster in recent years than that of their male counterparts.

Since Indian culture hinders women's access to jobs in stores, factories, and the public sector, the informal sector is particularly important for women. More women may be involved in undocumented or "disguised" wage work than in the formal labor force. There are estimates that over 90 percent of workingwomen are involved in the informal sector and not included in, official statistics. The informal sector includes jobs such as domestic servant, small trader, artisan, or field laborer on a family farm. Most of these jobs are unskilled and low paying and do not provide benefits to the worker. Although such jobs are supposed to be recorded in the census, undercounting is likely because the boundaries between these activities and other forms of household work done by women are often clouded thus, the actual labor force participation rate for women is likely to be higher than that which can be calculated from available data. Women working in the informal sector of India's economy are also susceptible to critical financial risks. Particularly vulnerable are the poorest of the poor. Should they become ill, lose their job, or be unable to continue working, they and their families may fall into debt and find themselves in the depths of poverty. At risk are millions of poor who depend on the income generated by one or more women in their household. These women do not have regular salaried employment with welfare benefits like workers in the organized sector of the labor market. Female workers tend to be younger than males. According to the 2001 census, the average age of all female workers was 33.6 compared with the male average of 36.5.These data are reported by local employment offices that register the number of people looking for work. The accuracy of, these data is questionable because many unemployed people may not register at these offices if there are no perceived benefits to registering. In addition, the offices operate more extensively in urban areas, thus likely undercounting unemployment in rural areas.

One would expect that as cultural impediments to work decrease, younger women would be the ones entering.the workforce; older women who have never worked in the formal sector are not likely to start working later in life. Throughout the economy, women tend to hold lower-level positions than men even when they have sufficient skills to perform higher-level jobs. Researchers have estimated that female agricultural laborers were usually paid 40 to 60 percent of the male wage. Even when women occupy similar positions and have similar educational levels, they earn just 80 percent of what men do, though this is better than in most developing countries.

The public sector hires a greater share of women than does the private sector, but wages in the public sector are less egalitarian despite laws requiring equal pay for equal work. There is evidence that suggests that technological progress sometimes has a negative impact on women's employment opportunities. When a new technology is introduced to automate specific manual labor, women may lose their jobs because they are often responsible for the manual duties. For instance, one village irrigated its fields through a bucket system in which women were very active. When the village replaced the manual irrigation system with a tube well irrigation system, women lost their jobs. Many other examples exist where manual tasks such as wheat grinding and weeding are replaced by wheat grinding machines, herbicides, and other modern technologies. These examples are not meant to suggest that women would be better off with the menial jobs rather they illustrate how women have been pushed out of traditional occupations.

Women may not benefit from jobs created by the introduction of new technology. New jobs (e.g., wheat grinding machine operator) usually go to men, and it is even rare for women to be employed in the factories producing such equipment. National Sample Survey data exemplify this trend. Since the 1970s, total female self-employment and regular employment have been decreasing as a proportion of total employment in rural areas, while casual labor has been increasing. Other data reinforce the conclusion that employment options for female agricultural workers have declined, and that many women seek casual work in other sectors characterized by low wages and low productivity. Other agricultural work includes workers involved with livestock, forestry, fishing and hunting, plantations, orchards, and related activities.

Even if a woman is employed, she may not have control over the money she earns, though this money often plays an important role in the maintenance of the household. In Indian culture women are expected to devote virtually all of their time, energy, and earnings to their family. Men, on the other hand, are expected to spend time and at least some of their earnings on activities outside the household. Research has shown that women contribute a higher share of their earnings to the family and are less likely to spend it on themselves. Research has suggested that as the share of the family income contributed by woman increases, so does the likelihood that she will manage this income. However, the extent to which women retain control over their own income varies from household to household and region to region. Many women still sought their husbands' permission when they wanted to purchase something for themselves. In northern India, where more stringent cultural restrictions are in place, it is likely that few women control family finances. Conditions of working women in India have improved considerably in the recent years. Ironically, despite the improvement in their status, they still find themselves dependent on men. It is because of the fact that man in patriarchal society has always wielded economic independence and power to take decision. Since the working woman earns an independent income in the same patriarchal set-up, where the basic infrastructure of society has hardly changed, though her own role within the same structure is passing through a transitional phase, it is but natural that she would remain vulnerable to exploitation even in her economically independent state. Society perhaps yet needs to accord due recognition to women to take the lead role and women, at the same time; need to be oriented vigorously towards assuming this role in the society.

## PROBLEMS OF GETTING EMPLOYMENT

Most of the women work to help their families in their economic disparities. However, the general impression of the society is to the contrary. When they search for a job, they have to compete with male candidates. The women in general suffer from some of the assumptions and prejudices which the authorities particularly the male, have towards them. The management feels that women are not serious or efficient workers. They put in less work and come only to pass time. As soon as they get married, they will go away. Again even if they continue after marriage, they will demand leave a number of times for domestic reasons. Maternity, childcare, transfer of husbands, work demands of the husband and family will make them give up jobs, play truant or become indifferent and efficient. For many such reasons the women candidates are not preferred. Some managements even think that the women may spoil the strict atmosphere of the office. In fact this type of discrimination with young girls in nothing but a crime against entire women community. Once they are selected, they are subjected to other types of oppressions. The stares and the banters of the male colleagues, their typical curiosity and their uncivilized and unwarranted remarks, "She is charming and that is why she is selected" etc. are some of these oppressive ways. If the young women mix freely with them they are misunderstood. If they keep themselves confined to the work alone, they are labeled as arrogant. If the boss appreciates their work and they enjoy the confidence of the authorities, they are scandalized. They crack jokes at them and pass cheap remarks which in fact are unfair to the young women and hurt them.

## EMPLOYED WOMEN-THEIR SATISFACTION AT HOME AND WORK

In the modern world, the women have to perform two challenging roles- one of the housewife and mother of a wage earner for supplementing the family income so that standard of living and quality of life of her family can be enhanced. In discharging her dual role at home and workplace and to strike an optimal balance amongst them, her satisfaction level varies. At work place, the different criteria for judging the satisfaction level included, behaviour of office mates, present status of job, nature of boss, work load, working hours etc. the comparison of satisfaction level shows that majority of teaching staff had high level of satisfaction than non-teaching staff as they had more income at their disposal and less family members in the home. Due to high education level, teaching staff had much of understanding between themselves for which they felt much satisfied than non-teaching staff. The important factors that were significantly correlated with the satisfaction level of respondents were found to be education, family type and total family income.

## PROBLEMS OF WORKING WOMEN

The crux of the problem of women's employment lies in the dilemma of her dual responsibilities in being a housewife, a mother as well as an employee and a producer of income for her family. Women are gradually realizing that they have personalities of their own as human beings. Their mission in life does not end with becoming good wives and wise mothers only, but also realizing that they are all equal members. Being a member of the family, each individual has a specific expectation from a woman. The in-laws have expectations from the daughter-in-law, the husband from the wives, and the children from their mother.

Working women's problems are aggravated by their multiple role expectations which we find in Indian society. Today, women have to perform multiple roles as of wife, mother, homemaker, worker and a citizen. A woman taking up a job outside, home also has to look after domestic work along with her official work. This dual responsibility has overburdened working women, thereby leading to multidimensional problems.

In our country joint family still exists in some form or the other. Parents-in-law still have many expectations from daughter-in-law in the matter of looking after their household affairs. In most cases husband also expects the same kind of attention from working as well as non working wife. She does not receive much consideration for the additional income. On the other hand, she does not carry out efficiently her role as a wife and mother apart from being accused of being insufficient and vain. She suffers from guilty feeling and finds herself torn between home and work.

Working women have a much larger area of social interaction. They get opportunity to meet more varied kinds of people. They have their own circle of colleagues. It may be found that due to their professional interests working women are also more often the members of voluntary associations. Therefore it is presumed that the area of informal activity of working women may be larger than that of the non working women.

After many centuries, once again, women are becoming productive members of the society. In addition to her traditional roles as wife, mother, guardian of the household and keeper of cultural traditions, she is now becoming a professional career woman. Industrialization has created an entirely different situation for the woman as a homemaker and a jobholder. Given the condition the woman work in addition to their household responsibilities, their perception regarding this situation becomes a question of considerable importance. Although, working women may feel that it is much harder to combine the dual responsibilities and they may also be quite aware of the influence that their work has on their family life. Another question that gains significance in this context is regarding the influence of outdoor work on the behavior pattern of women. Further, the question arise the consequences of a woman's employment.

Reddy (1986) explained that the problems of employed women are of three types- environmental, social and psychological. These problems emerge in two situations, that is, at home and at their workplace. Therefore, the problems of working women can be divided into two dimensions:

(a) Job Related Problems.

(b) Household Work Related Problems.

## *JOB RELATED PROBLEMS*

Consistent with the long-term trend the presence of women in work force continues to increase. The employment of women has opened up new vistas for women; shifting interest from household duties to work outside. While their work in the family goes unrewarded, employment in industries has made them economically independent and their monetary contribution is a substantial addition to household earning. As a result women have now come to work in all kind of professions, manual as well as blue collar and white collar jobs. With this expansion, employed women are facing problems in their job with regard to the changing nature of job, job adjustment, the way that work is organized including hours of work, job design, interpersonal factor, management style, working conditions and the organizational climate. The features like low pay, non-recognition and invisibilization of work often characterize women paid work.

Women work double the time than their counterparts. Attending to the daily household chores, looking after the children, family members and also working a full day in paid employment, she has no time to relax. Chronic fatigue, weakness are some of the results of such high level stress. Some other factors that contribute to stress related to job are monotonous work, poor ventilation, unfriendly working atmosphere and injustice at the workplace.

According to Mukhopadhyay (1999), "Psychological well being of employees at work has considerable impact on performance and productivity". However women are more susceptible to work related stress due to social and economic conditioning that shape their attitude and personality.

Gore (1988) stated that at the workplace women might face problems of relationship. He further explained that at the level of routine jobs they can leave their work worries in the office, but if they are working at a creative and competitive level or professional career, the demands mad on them can become heavy.

Another problem that the employed women face is that the efficiency of a working woman is always suspected. Despite being the same qualifications, authorities prefer a man that a woman especially in the middle cadre jobs with the doubt that whether she would be able to handle responsibilities take independent decisions, cope up with crisis and manage her duties. The co-workers in the office cannot mentally accept the superiority of the women workers. Women entering male dominated professions face problems such as the formation of an identify as a professional as well as women professional.

Stead (1985) analyzed that barriers for women in the workforce continue to present problems. When you talk with working women, they describe situations that sound like they might have come out of the dark ages. Many of today's professional women are no longer the first or the token woman in a given environment, but they may still occupy a career area in which women are few. They are still facing old stereotypes and the old problems in today's powerful work system.

Women employees face the problem of transfer in job placement as per ordered by the job authority, which becomes a critical situation for them, as they cannot get rid of family responsibilities. Thus, for the women in our country especially married working women, it becomes very difficult for them to join the job elsewhere. Hence, the problem is not with the women as officer or at any other post, but the very attitude of men and sometimes of women themselves, which cannot be changed, is the problem. Thus, in addition, the physical and psychological stress at job, together affect women employees health, morale and commitment adversely.

## *HOUSEHOLD WORK RELATED PROBLEMS*

In an Indian society it is only in the family that the role of a woman gains prominence. Although a woman has outside roles, yet it is her family and the home that hold her position as the focus of their activities. The participation of women in employment outside home has greatly changed their family lives.

Since primary responsibilities of the women revolve with home and children, so despite the arrangement made to ease their burden, they require to work at home in addition to their outdoor duties. This entails on them a much larger working day that they feel overworked and tired. Under such circumstances, it is quite liable to expect that when a woman has to work outdoor for 8-10 hours a day, she cannot pay the same amount of attention at her home, children and other family members as other non working women do.

Constant attention of the mother and her physical presence are considered important to provide healthy psychological environment for the development of a child's personality. When a mother of a school age children go out to work, naturally she has to leave her children in the care of someone else, which not only means an additional expenditure but also the feeling to the mother that she is neglecting her children. When a mother is working, the children also feel that they are neglected. They are not properly looked after and lack love and attention of their mothers. Further, they do not enjoy the facilities the other children do. Many a times, it also happens that the mother is not able to stay at home, when the child is sick. As it is considered that taking care of children is the entire responsibility of women. At this time, the child feels that she is not able to look after her sick child even though he/she is ill; who needs much more care and attention. She suffers from guilt consciousness and finds herself torn between the dual responsibilities.

Another aspect that may arise is that although the husbands do approve their wives work, yet at the same time it may hurt their male ego, thus resulting in conflict of authority between them. Carrying out almost single handedly all the duties and responsibilities of family, overstrain a working women and makes her tired and irritable, which in turn is liable to make her unpleasant and unenjoyable company to her husband, children and their family members.

Hofferth and Moore (1978) stated that although they gain power and contribute to family status, working wives did not obtain significantly more help in house work from their husband than do non-working wives. Thus, lack of cooperation form husband or other family members, inability to but modern gadgets or absence of servant or day care center; whatever is the cause of the problems of working women, it always ends up with some psychological problems, such as anxiety, restlessness, tension, guilty feeling, conflict with husband and children affect women's won health as well as satisfaction. The attitude of the husband and other family members towards the working women appeared to be a key factor influencing her work in the office and her duties at home. Professional working women have difficulties mainly in performing dual roles, acquiring co-operation form family members and compete with men to prove themselves.

## COPING WITH STRESS

When individuals experience stress, they adopt ways of dealing with it. An individual cannot remain in a continual state of tension so even if a deliberate and conscious strategy, is not utilized to deal with stress, some strategy is adopted. The word coping has been used mainly in two meanings, in a general meaning of ways of dealing with stress, or the effort to "master" conditions of harm, threat or challenge. We shall use the term coping in the first meaning (ways of dealing with stress), distinguishing with effective and ineffective coping.

## COPING UP STRATEGIES

Individuals cannot remain in a continuous state of tension. Even if a deliberate and conscious strategy is not adopted to deal with stress, some strategy is adopted; for example, to leave the conflicts and stress to take care of themselves. This is also a strategy, although the individual may not be aware of this. This is called avoidance coping strategy.

The word coping has two connotations in stress literature. It has been used to denote the way of dealing with stress, or the effort to 'master' conditions of harm, threat or challenge when a routine or automatic response is not readily available (Lazarus, 1974).

Coping traits refer to a disposition to respond in a specific way in situations that are stressful. Coping traits are thus stable characteristics of persons who transcend all stressful situations. Coping style implies a broader, more encompassing disposition. Traits and style are fundamentally similar ideas. Trait and style refer to a characteristic way of handling situations, they are stable tendencies on the basis of which inferences are drawn about how an individual will cope in some or all types of stressful situations. A person's coping style or disposition is typically assessed by personality tests, not by actual observation of what the person says or does in a particular stress situation.

The emphasis on process distinguishes this approach from other s which are trait-oriented. Psychologists have identified two major ways in which people cope with stress. In the first approach, a person may decide to suffer or deny the experienced stress, this is the passive approach. Or, a person may decide to face the realities of experienced stress and clarify the problem through negotiations with other members; this is the active approach (Pareek, 1983).

Coping can have an effect on three kinds of outcomes-psychological, social and physiological. From a psychological perspective, coping can have an effect on the person's morale (that is, the way one feels about oneself and one's life), emotional reaction, e.g., level of depression or anxiety, or the balance between positive trend and negative feelings (Bradburn, 1969), the incidence of psychiatric disorders and even performance. From a social perspective, one can measure its impact on functional effectiveness, such as employability, community involvement, and sociability (Renne, 1974), the effectiveness of interpersonal relationships, or the degree to which useful social roles are filled (and acting out anti-social behavior, etc., are avoided). From a physiological perspective, outcome includes short term consequences, such as the development and progression of a particular disease.

Approach or effective strategies of coping include efforts to measure physical and mental preparedness for coping (through physical exercise, yoga and meditation, diet management), creative diversions for emotional enrichment (music, art, theatre, etc.) and strategies of dealing with the basic problems.

## STRATEGIES FOR MANAGING JOB STRESS:

While many of the methods of preventing job stress need to be developed and supported by the organization, there are things that workers can do to help you better manage job stress.

*Here are 10 tips for dealing with the Stress from your Job:*

- *Put it in Perspective. Jobs are disposable:* Your friends, families, and health are not. If your employer expects too much of you, and it's starting to take its toll on you, start looking for a new job/new employer.

- *Modify your Job Situation:* If you really like your employer, but the job has become too stressful, ask about tailoring your job to your skills. And if you got promoted into a more stressful position that you just are not able to handle, ask about a lateral transfer or even a transfer back to your old job.
- *Get time Away:* If you feel the stress building, take a break. Walk away from the situation, perhaps walking around the block, sitting on a park bench, taking in a little meditative time. Exercise does wonders for the psyche. But even just finding a quiet place and listening to your iPod can reduce stress.
- *Fight through the Clutter:* Taking the time to organization your desk or workspace can help ease the sense of losing control that comes from too much clutter. Keeping to do list and then crossing things off it also helps.
- *Talk it Out:* Sometimes the best stress-reducer is simply sharing your stress with someone close to you. The act of talking it out and getting support and empathy from someone else is often an excellent way of blowing of steam and reducing stress. Have a support system of trusted people.
- *Cultivate Allies at Work:* Just knowing you have one or more co-workers who are willing to assist you in times of stress will reduce your stress level. Just remember to reciprocate and help them when they are in need.
- *Find Humor in the Situation:* When you or the people around you start taking things too seriously, find a way to break through with laughter. Share a joke or funny story.
- *Have Realistic Expectations:* While Americans are working longer hours, we can still only fit so much work into one day. Having unrealistic expectations for

what you can accomplish sets you up for failure — and increased stress.

- *Nobody is Perfect:* If you are one of those types that obsess over every detail and micromanage to make sure "everything is perfect," you need to stop. Change your motto to performing your best, and leave perfection to the gods.
- *Maintain a Positive Attitude (and avoid those without one):* Negativism sucks the energy and motivation out of any situation, so avoid it whenever possible. Instead, develop a positive attitude and learn to reward yourself for little accomplishments.

## JUSTIFICATION OF THE STUDY

Women's work and problems are closely related in number of ways. Women today are not only doing physical work in farms, factories, construction companies and industries but are also doing mental work by taking up employment in the jobs like administration, management, offices and courts. With the growing avenues, women facing various types of problems, which need to be sorted out and solved. This study deals with the problems and issues of working women and is lined with the efforts made towards employment of women. Working women should be encouraged to participate in the economic activities by the way of offering opportunities for advancement. Therefore, it becomes important to find out the problems of working women that hamper their participation in the gainful employment, and reduce their efficiency in the management of resources. Thus, this study will help in identifying the existing problems of working women.

There have been more studies conducted on the problems of women labour in factories, farms and construction sectors; however there has not been much literature dealing with the problems of educated and skilled working women. Professional women who have attempted to work with their potential capabilities and resources have entered the world of occupation and have made their carrier rapidly in this era. They are frequently caught in the situation, which are responsible for the overall adjustment of the women employees in their jobs. Hence, this study will also focus on some of the factors that are responsible for producing either physical or mental stress which could have adversely affected the health status of working women. Thus, by giving consideration to the findings of the study, the concerned institution can make to improve their professional efficiency and quality of work, which will directly leads to quality production.

The present study, therefore, will further be helpful in providing suggestions to protect and secure their potentialities by giving them certain facilities in terms of working conditions, management training for resource use, such as, time and energy, role adjustment, providing incentives and facilities offering family support.

Most of the working women face the problem of dual responsibilities whenever they take up employment outside their home. Despite, the seeming progress, women still occupy job and face problems related to their job and family. The self-analysis of these problems will help the women to know their own strength and weaknesses and thereby, can develop better ability to cope up with their dual responsibilities of job and family. Often these problems restrict women from taking benefit of employment opportunities and promotional avenues. Therefore, the suggestions for reducing the problems of working women will be helpful in providing possible solutions to some of their problems related to job and family.

Thus, the different dimensions of problems and issues related to working women have motivated the researcher to take up study on the problems of working women for the present research work.

## JUSTIFICATION OF THE STUDY IN RELATION TO THE DEPARTMENT OF EXTENSIXON AND COMMUNICATION

The Department of Extension and Communication is dealing with various issues related to women and great efforts in identifying and exploring various aspects related to the problems of working women. One of the major objectives of the department is to upgrade the status of women towards their development. So, there is a concern shown for betterment of women through availing gainful employment opportunities. The department also focuses on many projects and activities, thus, contributing in raising the status of women in society. Therefore, under rural and extension programmes of the department, the study will provide a platform to initiate welfare programmes for employed women. Seminars can be conducted on different aspects related to women and vocation such as, stress management, vocational counseling, quality management resource etc.

The department is also offering courses related to women's issues in its curriculum like women in changing India at undergraduate level and women and development and women in administration at post graduate level, which deals with the problems and issues of the women, related to the work and exploring these aspects in relation to women and employment. Thus, adding to the knowledge, information and modifications for the development of the above courses.

The study will create awareness among the extension workers, educators and social workers about multifarious problems of women workers related to various aspects of their life. This will also help the concerned authorities to initiate welfare programmes for the women workers such as health check-ups, vocational and personal counseling, conducting seminars and training programmes for better management of human resources to increase work efficiency. The concerned authorities can discuss the findings of these studies with the women employees and help them to make adjustment in their dual role of a homemaker and that of working women.

## JUSTIFICATION OF THE VARIABLES

Since, there are various factors, which can affect the extent of problems of working women; it was decided to include the following variables in the present study.

### *AGE OF THE RESPONDENT*

Age affects the extent of problems faced by the working women in their job as well as in the family. Young women may have more energy to attend the dual roles. Conversely, the young workingwomen may have more responsibilities of young children and they may not be well adjusted to the dual responsibilities. This may create a different set of problems for the younger and older working women. On the other hand, old working women may be more confident and self dependent. They may have less family responsibilities as their children are grown up. They may be well adjusted to dual responsibilities of job and family with their through experience. However, they may have more physical health problems. It may be possible that due to lack of experience, the young working women may face more problems than the old working women. So, it would be interesting to find out all these variations in working women with different age. Thus, age has been taken as a variable.

### *TYPE OF FAMILY*

The problems of working women may vary according to the type of family. The working women from nuclear family may have more household responsibilities due to which they may face difficulty in carrying out the dual responsibility of job and family. Moreover, the working women from nuclear family may have more worries regarding the proper care of their children because of which they may not be able to concentrate on their job demands. On the other hand, working women from joint family may face less problems due to division of house hold work with other family members and thus may have less worries. So, this may create a different set of problems for the working women from nuclear and joint family.

### *EXPERIENCE*

In general, it is believed that people get adjusted more and more with the passage of time and experience. Being more experienced, they have more confidence, may commit lesser mistakes and may handle the situation efficiently. Therefore, they may rarely face the problems. Although, the working women with many years of employment may have more experience of work. They may be well adjusted to the dual responsibilities. Thus, they may face fewer problems. However, working women with less numbers of years of employment may be passing through adjustment period due to working. They may not have developed techniques of problem solving which arise due to dual responsibilities. They may not be able to visualize the problems and difficulties. It may be possible that they may feel overloaded with work, and as a result commit more mistakes, and several problems may arise at work place. So it is felt important to study the problems of the working women related to their job and family with respect to their number of years of employment.

### *DISTANCE FROM WORKPLACE*

It also affects the extent of problems faced by working women. If there is a long distance between the working place of a woman and her residence, she may spend more time in traveling. This means she is left with less time to spend at home. So she may not be able to serve the family members satisfactorily. Thus, it may lead to tension and frustration for her as well as for her family members. However, women with less distance from the workplace may find easy to manage household work, may face no difficulty of transportation and may easily reach at work place. Therefore, the distance from workplace will show variation in the problems of working women.

## OBJECTIVES OF THE STUDY

1. To study the *problems faced by working women* in the city of Baroda.
2. To study the problems of working women *in relation to* their-
   (a) Job related problems
   (b) Household work related problems
3. To study the differences *in the overall problems* of working women with respect to the following variables.
   - Age
   - Experience
   - Type of family
   - Distance from workplace

4. To study the differences in the *Job related problems* of working women with respect to the following variables:
   - Age
   - Experience
   - Type of family
   - Distance from workplace
5. To study the differences in the *Household work related problems* of working women with respect to the following variables:
   - Age
   - Experience
   - Type of family
   - Distance from workplace
6. To study the *coping up strategies* used by the working women to manage stress.
7. To obtain the *suggestions* to reduce the problems of working women.

## ASSUMPTION OF THE STUDY

1. Working women use coping up strategies to manage stress due to their multiple roles.

## NULL HYPOTHESES OF THE STUDY

1. There will be no significant differences *in the overall problems* of working women with respect to the following variables:
   - Age
   - Experience
   - Type of family
   - Distance from workplace
2. There will be no significant differences in the *Job related problems* of working women with respect to the following variables:
   - Age
   - Experience
   - Type of family
   - Distance from workplace
3. There will be no significant differences in the *Household work related problems* of working women with respect to the following variables:
   - Age
   - Experience
   - Type of family
   - Distance from workplace

## DELIMITATION OF THE STUDY

The study is delimited to only the problems of working women of Baroda who are doing job and get salary for their work.

## OPERATIONAL DEFINITION

*Working Women:* Working women refers to the women working on economically gainful occupation for any number of hours a day at a particular place.

# 2

# REVIEW OF LITERATURE

The present study aims at studying the problems of working women from Baroda in the year 2008-09. With the expansion of better educational and professional opportunities the presence of women in organized sector is very much visible. Hence, both the conceptual and empirical literature was available.

The literature reviewed in this chapter has been divided into following sections:

- Conceptual Review
- Empirical Review

## CONCEPTUAL REVIEW

### *RESEARCHES CONDUCTED ON WORKING WOMEN IN INDIA*

Anand (2003) pointed out in the article titled "Working Women: Issues and Problems" that through development policies and performance have created a positive impact in women's position in the society but they are facing many problems and difficulties at home and working place. Some major issues and problems indicate women status which is as follow-

- Women worker perform dual role in society relating to production and reproduction leads to over-burdened life.

- Their contribution to the family, economy and national economy remains largely invisible and undervalued.
- Working for a longer time in unhygienic conditions affects working women's health.
- Lack of integrated approach in macro policies in tackling women issues.
- Unchecked exploitation of women in houses, working places and public places.

Arya (1990) has discussed some problems arising from the women's working status. The working wife herself in confused and the attitude of her husband and society in ambivalent. She wants to be respected as a sincere and efficient worker but they do not want her to be independent and only expect her to be obedient submissive wife. This thinking pattern has caused multiple socio-psychological problems.

Banerji and Sen (2000) has discussed that the treatment of superiors towards women employees does not alone determine the status of women in office. As a women employed in an office has not only superiors but also colleagues and subordinates. When the male colleagues and subordinates do not treat the women equally with other male staff members by giving respect and cooperation, the women would not be to work as efficiently as she could. If the treatment of male colleagues towards employed women is not considered the real picture of the status of women cannot be established. They further reported that the respect earned from the colleagues can be measured on account of the aspects

- Cooperation form colleagues.
- Appreciation of good work.
- Recognition from colleagues.
- Behavior expressing resentment.
- Being given all unpleasant work.

Bhoite (1988) undertook an investigation to survey the familial problems of employed women in lower middle class category. She found that no servants to help, no modern gadgets to save labour and time, no help from relatives or husband, responsibilities of young children, pressure of religious rituals and full time job outside the home were the main problems faced by these employed women.

Gore (1988) stated that at the workplace women may face problems of relationship. The married women are doing two jobs though are paid for only one. Gore explained that at the level of routine jobs or clerical jobs they can leave their work worries in the office, but if they are working at the creative, competitive level in an executive or professional career the demands made on them can become heavy. They are at a disadvantage competing with men who are not expected to carry any domestic responsibilities. He also writes that the idea that a man is totally absorbed in his work and can leave the home entirely to his wife is socially accepted: the idea of woman leaving the home totally to her husband-even if the children are grown up-is still not accepted.

Kapoor (1984) attempted to study the job satisfaction/ stress and coping styles of educated mothers gainfully employed outside the home. The findings of the study revealed that the husbands were satisfied to have working wife. Major reasons for objection were neglect of household, less care of children and burden of household responsibilities. Among the psychological problems, the study revealed that anxiety was the most common followed by emotional stress, depression and job satisfaction. It was further revealed that the major physical problem was headache. The findings also showed that the job satisfaction decreased and stress increased with increasing occupational status.

Lalitha (1982), in the study on Status of employment of women in India, found that the employment has contributed significantly to raise the status of women in the family and that the employed woman has higher status in the family that her unemployed counterpart. It was also reported that employed women received ample cooperation from male members in office. They were also recognized and appreciation for their good work in office.

Parikh and Shah (1994), in an article- "Women Managers in Transition: from home to corporate offices stated that although the Indian family setting provides eventual support to women working in organization, it also creates tremendous guilt and stress. At each new step the women take she is confronted with the process of being a victim and martyr. Her own ambition, achievement and improvement in work generate threats and anxieties in the significant role holders of the family, the husband, in laws and children. The husband puts her in the middle of two systems and questions her loyalty to the family setting. The in laws demand the traditional ideal role model of daughter-in-law, a traditional mother who is forever present at all times. Thus, the women executives carry burden and stress at their job.

Patel (1988) discussed that qualification being the same the authorities prefer a man than a woman especially in upper cadre with the doubt whether she would be able to handle many subordinates, take independent decisions, cope up with crisis and manage her duties. The co-workers in the office cannot mentally accept the superiority of the women workers. Women boss face some other kind of problems too. The subordinate males do not like to accept the authority of a woman. This type of problems may not last long.

Rath (1987) on the basis of a sample of Cuttack city observed that the employed women living in nuclear families had better adjusted married life that those living in joint families. Attitudinal changes were found from the employed women of the study when their opinions were asked for the solution of their problems. It was thus revealed that the working women had opined that all the work and responsibilities should be distributed among all the family members. They also wanted that men should improve their attitudes towards the working women. To lead a happy and prosperous family and to improve their status, the husband, other members of the family and the society should cooperate with her in every walk of life.

Reddy (1986) explained that the problems of working women are of three types: environmental, social and psychological. These problems emerge in two situations- at home and at work place. The problems are mainly two fold.

One is of inner conflict due to dual commitment and concern and the other is practical difficulty of combining work commitment with their role at home. Reddy further explained that the educated working women have now become assertive, more equality conscious and independent, but majority of husbands do not accept the changed life pattern of their working wives. Carrying out almost single handedly all the duties and responsibilities of home, overstrains a working woman and makes her tired and irritable, which in turn is liable to make her an unpleasant and unenjoyable company to her husband and children.

Swarnalata (1986) in a study with women IAS officers revealed that, they faced the problems of adjustment with the surroundings, jealousy of male officers, problems of being accepted, the twin problems of job and family, and the problem of over protective behavior of the bosses, only in the beginning of the career. But with the passage of time and as they gained experience, few difficulties came in the way of their working. These women officers also felt the problem of field posting which needed lot of touring. The problem of accepting the junior post to satisfy the ego of the husband was also felt by some of the officers. Some of the officers found it a problem to work with senior women officers as they were very rude in their behavior. A sample of working women of varied socio-economic and cultural background of Madras city was studied by Mani (1987). The findings did pinpoint some of the problems faced by these women. 80 percent of the husbands expected their wives to hand over the complete salary to them. 68 percent felt that home and children were neglected, though the standard of living is slightly better. 62 percent insisted that their wives should be at home between 5:30 and 6:00 p.m., irrespective of the pressure of the work in the office. The findings of the study further revealed that 49 percent of the women also felt that their first priority was only home (husband and children) and they did not like to stay in the office after 5 p.m., at any cost. The data also indicated that these women did not like to go out with colleagues and friends like their male counterparts but only with members of their own family.

Sinha and Prabha (1988) attempted to examine the status of working women who were gainfully employed in two sectors: the blue collar and the white collar occupations. For the purpose of the study status was conceptualized as multi-facet Construct and denoted not only the "Conjunctions of rights and duties" as reflected in women's different roles as mother, wife, daughter-in-law but also the degree of her subordination at home, her education and her degree of participation in public life, her role in decision making in family affairs and herself perceived status in the home. As far as respondents' restrictions on activities were concerned it was revealed that the married women engaged in blue collar jobs were generally not allowed to talk to husband in presence of family adults, have male friends whom husband disliked. The white collar working women encountered restrictions mostly on having male friends, female friends whom husband disliked and also on going out for recreation with friends. A comparative analysis revealed that in almost all activities, the white collar working women encountered greater restriction that those of blue collar working women. However, the later category faces greater restriction on one activity: they do not talk to husband in presence of elder members of the family. The findings also revealed that wives enjoy less power in respect of economic activities of their families like purchase of clothing. The white collar women were allowed to work outside but were restricted in spending their earnings at will.

Sundaram, et. Al. (1984), undertook a study with 80 working women of an urban area of Tamil Nadu, and found that the entire working women community without any single exception lived in pucca and decent houses with good ventilation facilities. It was revealed that nine-tenth of them were found to possess fans and radios. The researcher found that that the standard of living of these working women was far superior. Majority of them employed maid servants to assist them in their domestic work. The advantages of their employment were: additional income to the family, better status in society, and moral satisfaction.

## *RESEARCH CONDUCTED OUTSIDE INDIA*

Research studies related to the present investigation which was carried out in foreign countries are presented below.

The investigation undertaken by Coverman (1985) showed persistence of the unequal contribution by males and females to the division of labour in household work and child care. It was revealed that males still spent more time than female in work outside home and make a far smaller contribution than their wives to child care and household responsibilities.

In a survey by the Japanese Prime Minister's Office reported by Kyodo report, Tokyo (1990), it was found that a majority of women (56%) now believed that household chores should be shared by their husbands, up from 45% in a similar survey in 1983. The men did not share the new view. However, with over half (53%) saying housework and child cares are primarily the responsibility of woman. The nationwide survey conducted by interviewing 3,677 men and women between ages 20 and 60, indicated that while women feel they have more job opportunities that before, lack of adequate child care programmes and facilities for the elderly continue to impede employment. Traditional attitudes that woman belongs at home and unequal opportunities for job training promotions were also among the obstacles cited.

Both the above studies conducted in 80's and 90's showed that no matter how far women were coming out of their house for employment, the husbands still considered the household responsibilities were to be of women. The employed women also felt the absence of support services to solve their problems adequately.

## EMPIRICAL REVIEW

## *RESEARCHES CONDUCTED ON WORKING WOMEN IN INDIA*

A number of researches were conducted in India on various issues of employment of women during the years of 1970 and 1980. The findings reflecting the positive changes of women's employment arc highlighted.

Agrawal (1988) conducted a study on urban employed women-teachers of colleges and universities and Doctors in Meerut city. The aim was to find out that how far the gender equality concept has been inculcated in the members of the family-husbands, wives, children and parent-in-law, how far household responsibility, child care and family decision are being equally shared between husband and wife. He also studied the factors influencing the desired goal of equality of sexes. Interview cum questionnaire method of data collection was used for the study. The sample consisting of 90 teachers out of a total of 257 and 10 doctors out of 103 randomly selected consisting both rural and urban background. Rating scale was used. Quantitative as well as qualitative analysis were computed with frequency and percentages. Correlation between variables and status indices was found out. Findings of the study revealed that, although traditionally it was women's domain of work a little change in men's mind is creeping in and a small percentage of husbands had started helping wives in household work. It was also revealed, that nuclear family structure went in favour of the equality of husband and wife in comparison to joint family structure. A higher percentage of husbands in urban families help wives in household work as compared to those in rural families. The study also revealed that equal education of husband and wife was found to have a positive relation with the sharing of household work by husbands. It was also found that higher the role of women in the economy of the family, higher was her status. There was a positive relationship between high education of wives and their contribution in child centred decisions. As far as profession was concerned it was revealed, that husbands and wives having same profession were more co-operative than those who had different professions. One encountering and important finding of the study revealed, that some husbands though small in percentage (30%), supported women's own development.

Christopher (2001) conducted a study on role satisfaction and role conflicts among married working women in the organized sector of Tirupattur town. The objectives were to study the role satisfaction and the role conflicts existing among married working women in their family and work force. The sample of the study consisted of 46 married working women from state government, central government, quasi governmental and non-governmental institution. Sample was drawn through simple random lottery method. A structured interview schedule was used for data collection. He found that more than half (56.5 percent) of the respondents expressed dissatisfaction with regard to the time spend in showering parental love and affection towards their children, majority of the respondents (82.6 percent) got help in performing household work, and majority of the married working women (80.8 percent) have expressed satisfaction in their role performance at work in the areas like duration of work, professional fulfillment, equal status and good relationship with the superiors. Thus, to conclude the data reveals that higher the satisfaction in the role performance in the family, higher is the satisfaction in the role performances at work.

Deshpande (1992) studied the family adjustment pattern of married working women in Baroda city. The objectives of the study were to study how the working women are able to adjust between their family life and career life, to study the problems faced by these women in their family adjustment and to study the attitudes of family members towards the dual roles performed by the working women. The sample of the study consisted of 75 married working women from Lakhanpal National Limited and Hindustan Fashion House Limited through lottery sampling method. An interview schedule was used for data collection. He found that Few respondents were helped in household work by their husbands, nearly sixty percent of the respondents were of the opinion that their children disliked mother being employed.

Dubey (1982) carried out a study on working women and their problems in the New India Industries Limited, Baroda. The ultimate objective of the study aims at knowing how much of adjustment a women worker has to do work in a non-traditional way of earning and supporting the family income. The sample of the study consisted of 50 women from New

India Industries Limited through stratified sampling method. An interview schedule was used for data collection. He found in his study that majority of the respondents had conflict with their husband pertaining to children.

Mathews (1990) carried out a psycho-social study of working women with the objectives to know the problems of working women related to social, economic and psychological aspect due to working conditions and to know how much adjustment a women worker has to do. The data were collected through an interview schedule from 50 female teachers of The M.S. University of Baorda by simple random sampling method. The findings of his study were that most of the respondents agreed that they felt the need for leisure time activity for personal growth and development and majority of the working women got the cooperation of their colleagues at workplace.

Mukhopadhyay (1999) studied the stress in the lives of the working women and coping mechanism. The purpose of the study was to analyses some correlates of social and psychological conditioning and their likely impact on women's mental health. The sample consisted of mixed group of 45 middle and junior level women administrators, managers and professionals from government organizations and was interviewed on job related variable like work culture, peer subordinate relations, support mechanism and facilitating behavior of their bosses. The findings of his study were that dual roles in family and workplace often make women more tense and Prolonged role ambiguity and role conflict leads to reduced job satisfaction and higher anxiety level.

Murty (2001) conducted a study on problems of employed educated women in a few selected of Indian Economy in Ujjain City of Madhya Pradesh. The objectives of the study were to evaluate the working and non working conditions and atmosphere of the educated and skilled women workers and to find out their problems. The sample of the study consisted of 100 working women from teaching medicine, engineering and administration through stratified random sampling. Questionnaire interview method was adopted for data collection. It was found in this study that Fifty five percent of the women reported that their children are not getting desired attention due to their employment and high majority of the working women feel that they are overburdened due to their dual responsibilities at home and job.

Rawat (2004) carried out a study of the problems of working women from the selected public sectors of Baroda city in the year 2003-04. The objective of the study was to study the problems of working women from the selected public sectors of Baroda city in relation to their job and Family. The sample of the study consisted of 100 women employees in the middle cadre jobs from the four public sectors of Baroda city. The purposive sampling method was used to select the sample of the study. A Structured Questionnaire was used for data collection. It was found out that there were overall more problems faced by the working women from the selected public sectors of Baroda city.

From the foregoing Indian studies reviewed so far it was evident that employed women of Indian society faced the problem of non co-operation, non-acceptance and objectionable treatment from the male community i.e., the husbands at home and the colleagues at office. Jobs are opened to women but not the conducive environment through right behavior of people as well as proper facilities and services to support correspondingly.

# 3

# METHODOLOGY

The present research was undertaken to study the problems of working women of Baroda in the year 2008-09. In this chapter, methods and techniques employed to study the problems of working women have been described.

- Description of Population.
- Selection of Sample and Sampling method.
- Construction of Research Tool.
- Validity of Research Tool.
- Pretesting of the Tool.
- Collection of Data.
- Scoring and Categorization.
- Plan of Statistical Analysis.

## DESCRIPTION OF POPULATION

To study the problems of working women of Baroda city of Gujarat State, the working women in the year 2008-09 were taken as population for the study.

## SELECTION OF SAMPLES AND SAMPLING METHOD

The sample of the present study consisted of 120 working women from Baroda. The Purposive Sampling method was used to select the sample of the study.

## CONSTRUCTION OF RESEARCH TOOL

The Questionnaire for collecting the information for the present study was constructed from various books, journals, and papers, personal experience of the investigation and also through discussion with experts. The various sections of the questionnaire were developed according to the objectives. The detail description of each section of the questionnaire is presented here. Finally a Structured Questionnaire was developed by the investigator to study the problems of working women from Baroda in the year 2008-09. The Questionnaire was in English as well as in Gujarati language. (Appendix I, II)

The investigator constructed the tool after reviewing the related literature form the journals, articles, reports, books and dissertations. The investigator had visited Women Studies and Research Centre, Smt. Hansa Mehta Library, Reading and Documentation Centre of Department of Extension and Communication, The M.S. University, Baroda.

The Questionnaire was divided into four sections. The first section consisted of the Background Information with the sub section containing statements related to the working conditions. The Second Section consisted of the Problems related to the Paid work and Problems in carrying out responsibilities of household work. The Third Section included Coping up Strategies used by working women to manage stress and the Fourth Section consisted of the list of statements expressing the suggestions to reduce the problems of working women.

## VALIDITY OF THE TOOL

The Questionnaire was given to experts for checking the appropriateness of the tool for its content, response system and the language used. Content of the questionnaire to see the coverage of the objectives under study, Clarity and ambiguity in the use of language and Format of the questionnaire.

The experts had suggested certain minor changes in the questionnaire which were incorporated before pretesting the questionnaire. Changes were made in the Questionnaire on the basis of suggestions and comments received from the experts.

## PRETESTING OF THE RESEARCH TOOL

Pre-Testing of the tool was done to check the clarity of the language and to find out the time required by the respondents to fill up the Questionnaire. The questionnaire was translated into two languages English and Gujarati by the respondents. The translated questionnaires were distributed to ten working women of different professions during the month of October-November 2008 which were excluded from the final data. The data collected for pre-testing were analyzed and final changes were made in the Questionnaire.

## COLLECTION OF DATA

The data was collected in the month of November- December 2008. The investigator had personally distributed the Questionnaires and collected Data.

## SCORING AND CATEGORIZATION

Scoring and Categorization of the Independent and Dependent Variables.

The variables which were not categorized in the questionnaire were clustered into categories to test the hypotheses.

**Table 1**
**Categorization of the Independent Variables**

| *Variables* | *Basis* | *Category* |
|---|---|---|
| Age | 20-29 Yrs. | Young |
| | 30-39 Yrs. | Middle |
| | 40 Yrs and Above | Old |
| Type of family | — | Joint |
| | | Nuclear |
| | | Extended |
| Experience | 1-6 Yrs | Novice |
| | 7-12 Yrs | Less |
| | 13 Yrs and Above | More |
| Distance from workplace | Upto 2 kms | Near |
| | 3 kms to 6 kms | Fairly Distant |
| | 7 kms or more | Distant |

**Table 2**
**Scoring and Categorization of Other Background Information**

| *Variables* | *Basis* | *Category* |
|---|---|---|
| Educational Qualification | Post Graduate and Post Graduate Diploma Holder | Post Graduate |
| | Graduate and Diploma Holder | Graduate |
| | HSC Pass and below 12th Pass | Under Graduate |
| Family size | 1-3 members | Small |
| | 4-6 members | Medium |
| | 7 members or more | Large |
| Monthly income of the respondent | Upto Rs. 10,000 | Low |
| | Rs. 10,000 or more | More |
| Number of earning members | Upto 2 members | Few |
| | 3 or more members | Many |
| Family Income | Below Rs 19,000 | Average |
| | Above Rs. 19,000 | More than average |
| Job Designation | Engineer, Advocate, Administrative officer, Supervisor, Accountant, Financial Accountant, College Teacher, | Class I |
| | School Teacher, NGO Worker, Clerks, Nurses, Telesales | Class II |
| | Executives, Micro Biologist, Attendant, Data Preparation Assistant, Accountant Assistant, Private Secretary | Class III |
| Working hours | 3-5 hours¦ | Less than normal |
| | 6-8 hours¦ | Normal |
| | More than 8 hours | More than normal |
| Mode of Transport | k | Personal |
| | | Conveyance provided by Office |
| | | Public Transport |
| | | By walking |

## JOB RELATED PROBLEMS AND HOUSEHOLD WORK RELATED PROBLEMS OF WORKING WOMEN

The Two point response system was used to measure the problems of working women related to their paid work and household work. The total number of items was 70 respectively. The items were scored separately as follows:

| *Level of Response* | *Weightage* |
|---|---|
| Yes | 2 |
| No | 1 |

## COPING UP STRATEGIES USED BY WORKING WOMEN TO MANAGE THE STRESS

The Four point response system was used to measure the coping up strategies used by working women. The total number of items was 31. The items were scored separately as follows:

*For positive responses, the items were scored as:*

| *Level of Response* | *Weigtage* |
|---|---|
| Strongly Agree | 4 |
| Agree | 3 |
| Disagree | 2 |
| Strongly Disagree | 1 |

*For Negative responses, the items were scores as:*

| *Level of Response* | *Weigtage* |
|---|---|
| Strongly Agree | 1 |
| Agree | 2 |
| Disagree | 3 |
| Strongly Disagree | 4 |

## SUGGESTIONS TO REDUCE THE PROBLEMS OF WORKING WOMEN

The three point response system was used to reduce the problems of working women. The total number of items was 23. The items were scored separately as follows:

| *Level of Response* | *Weigtage* |
|---|---|
| Great Extent | 3 |
| Some Extent | 2 |
| Less Extent | 1 |

### *Itemwise Intensity Indices*

Itemwise Intensity Indices were calculated for both Job and Household work related aspects, coping up Strategies and Suggestions.

*Formula used for Item wise intensity Indices was:*

$$\text{Item wise Intensity Indices} = \frac{\textit{Total score for an item}}{\textit{Total number of the Respondents}}$$

*Formula for ANOVA ('F' test) used in the study:*

$$F = \frac{\textit{Large Variance}}{\textit{Small Variance}}$$

$$or = \frac{\textit{Between Group Variance}}{\textit{Within Group Variance}}$$

*Between Group Variance* = Variance in the mean of each group from the total mean of all variance groups.

*Within Group Variance* = Average variability of scores within group

## PLAN FOR STATISTICAL ANALYSIS

**Table 3**
**Different Statistical Measures Used for the Analysis of the Data**

| *Purposes Measures* | *Statistical* |
|---|---|
| *Background Information* of the respondents | Percentages |
| *Job related Problems* and *Household work related Problems* of working women | Intensity Indices |
| Differences in the overall problems of working women with respected to the *selected variables.* | F-Test (ANOVA) |
| Differences in the *Job related problems* of working women with respected to the selected variables. | F-Test (ANOVA) |
| Differences in the *Household work related problems* of working women with respected to the selected variables. | F-Test (ANOVA) |
| *Coping up Strategies* to manage stress of working women | Intensity Indices |
| *Suggestions* to reduce the problems of working women | Intensity Indices |

# 4

# FINDINGS AND DISCUSSION

The present chapter deals with the findings of the study which are as follows:

I. Background Information

II. Other Background Information

III. Problems of Working Women

(a) *Job Related Problems of Working Women*

(b) *Household Work Related Problems of Working Women*

IV. Differences in the Problems of Working Women with Respected to the Selected Variables

V. Variablewise Differences in the Overall Problems of Working Women

(a) *Variablewise Differences in the Job Related Problems of Working Women*

(b) *Variablewise Differences in the Household Work Related Problems of Working Women*

VI. Coping up Strategies used by Working Women to manage Stress

VII. Suggestions to Reduce the Problems of Working Women

## BACKGROUND INFORMATION OF THE RESPONDENTS

Table–1 reveals that forty percent of the respondents were from younger age group whereas nearly thirty six percent of the respondents were from the old age group and more than twenty percent of the respondents were from the middle age group.

**Table 1**
**Percentage Distribution of the Respondents According to the *Variables***

*N=120*

| *Variables* | *Frequency* | *Percentages (%)* |
|---|---|---|
| **Age** | | |
| Younger | 49 | 40.8 |
| Middle | 28 | 23.3 |
| Old | 43 | 35.8 |
| **Type of Family** | | |
| Joint | 45 | 37.5 |
| Nuclear | 73 | 60.8 |
| Extended | 2 | 1.7 |
| **Experience** | | |
| 1-6 years | 62 | 52 |
| 7-12 years | 22 | 18 |
| 13 years and above | 36 | 30 |
| **Distance from the Workplace** | | |
| Upto 2 kms | 46 | 38.3 |
| 3-6 kms | 42 | 35.0 |
| 7 kms or more | 32 | 26.7 |

Further the table 4 reveals that majority sixty one percent of the respondents were from the nuclear family whereas more than thirty percent of the respondents were from the joint family and nearly two percent of the respondents were from the extended family.

## VARIABLE WISE DISTRIBUTION OF THE RESPONDENTS

It reveals that fifty two percent of the respondents reported less years of experience, eighteen percent of the respondents reported few years of experience whereas thirty percent of the respondents reported more years of experience.

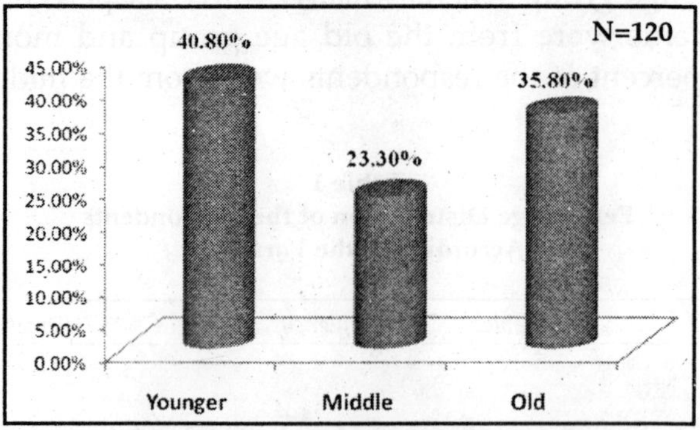


**Figure: 1 Percentage Distribution of the Respondents According to their *Age***

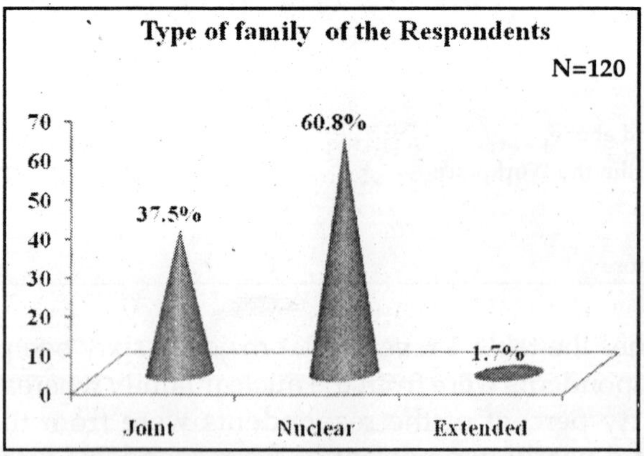


**Figure: 2 Percentage Distribution of the Respondents According to their *Type of Family***

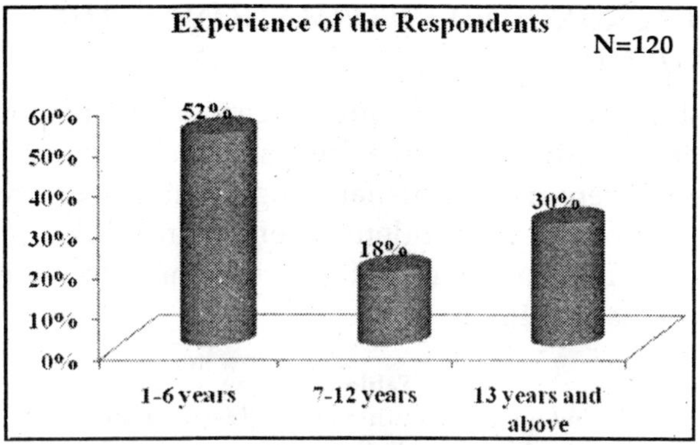


**Figure: 3 Percentage Distribution of the Respondents According to their *Experience***

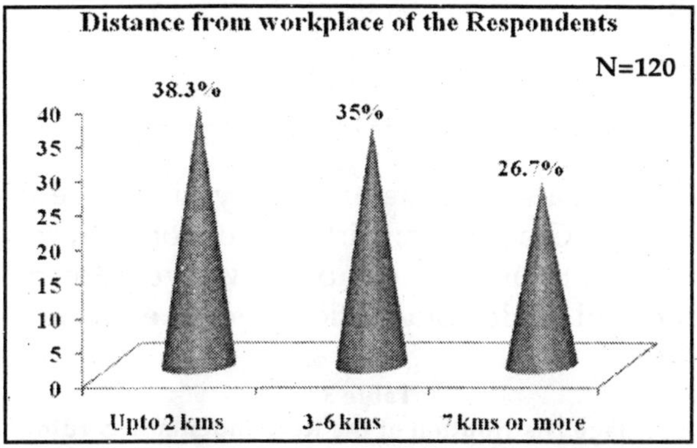


**Figure: 4 Percentage Distribution of the Respondents According to their *Distance from Workplace***

Furthermore, it was revealed from table 4 that thirty eight percent of the respondents had Less Distance, thirty five percent of the respondents had Few Distance whereas twenty six percent of the respondents had More Distance from home to the workplace.

Thus, majority of the respondents belonged to younger age group, had nuclear family, had less number of years of employment and had less distance from home to the workplace.

## *OTHER BACKGROUND INFORMATION OF THE RESPONDENTS*

Table 2 shows that nearly ninety percent of the respondents were from Hindu religion whereas five percent of the respondents were from Christian religion and very few only two percent of the respondents were from Shikh religion whereas nearly two percent of the respondents were from Muslim and Jain religion.

**Table 2**
**Percentage Distribution of the Respondents According to their Religion**

*N=120*

| Religion | Frequency | Percentages (%) |
|---|---|---|
| Hindu | 107 | 89.2 |
| Mulsim | 2 | 1.7 |
| Shikh | 3 | 2.5 |
| Christian | 6 | 5.0 |
| Any Other: (Jain) | 2 | 1.7 |

Table 3 reveals that majority fifty six percent of the respondents had Graduation; thirty percent of the respondents had Post Graduation whereas only twelve percent of the respondents had Under Graduation level of education.

**Table 3**
**Percentage Distribution of the Respondents According to their Educational Qualification**

*N=120*

| *Educational Qualification* | *Frequency* | *Percentages (%)* |
|---|---|---|
| Post Graduate | 37 | 30.8 |
| Graduate | 68 | 56.7 |
| Under Graduate | 15 | 12.5 |

Table 4 revealed that High majority eighty nine percent of the respondents had Own or Self Possessed house whereas less than ten percent of the respondents had Rented house and only two percent of the respondents had Quarters provided by the Employers.

**Table 4**
**Percentage Distribution of the Respondents According to their Residence**

N=120

| *Residence* | *Frequency* | *Percentages (%)* |
|---|---|---|
| Own or Self Possessed house | 107 | 89.2 |
| Rented house | 10 | 8.3 |
| Quarter provided by the employer | 3 | 2.5 |

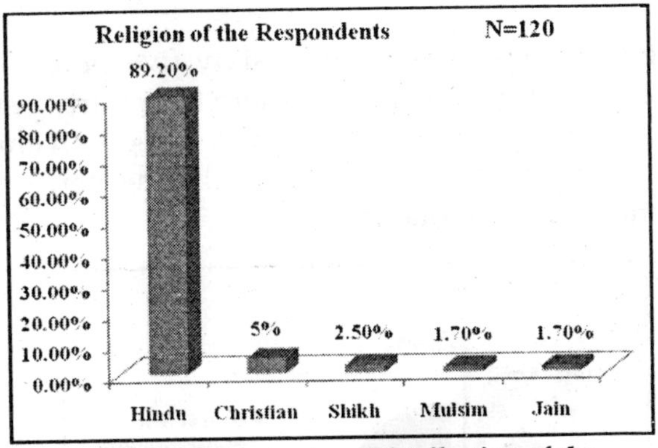


**Figure 5: Percentage Distribution of the Respondents According to their *Religion***

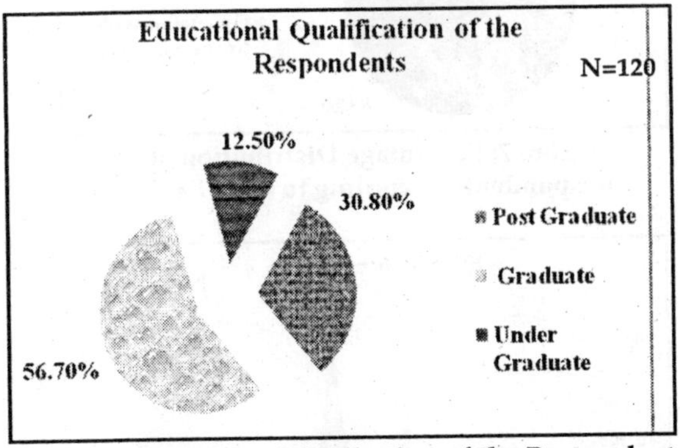


**Figure 6: Percentage Distribution of the Respondents According to their *Educational Qualification***

It is revealed from the table 5 that more than sixty percent of the respondents belonged to Medium sized family, little more than twenty five percent of the respondents belonged to Small sized family whereas only ten percent of the respondents belonged to large sized family.

**Table 5**
**Percentage Distribution of the Respondents According to their *Family Size***

*N=120*

| *Family Size* | *Frequency* | *Percentages (%)* |
|---|---|---|
| 1-3 member | 32 | 26.7 |
| 4-6 members | 76 | 63.3 |
| 7 members or more | 12 | 10 |

Table 6 reveals that majority sixty five percent of the Respondents were married, little more than thirty percent of the respondents were unmarried, and three percent of the respondents were Widow whereas only one percent of the respondents were separated.

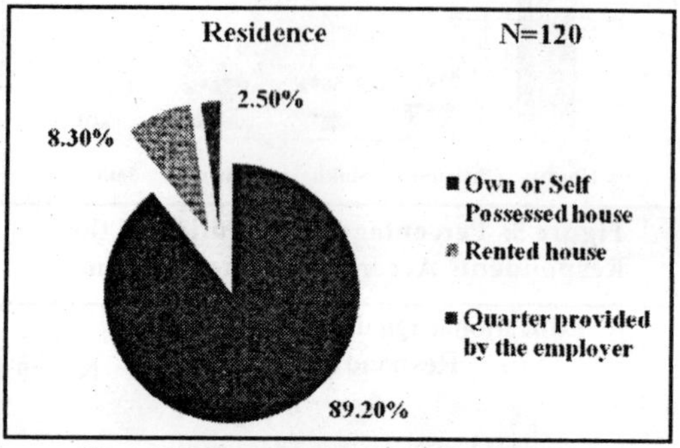


**Figure 7: Percentage Distribution of the Respondents According to their *Residence***

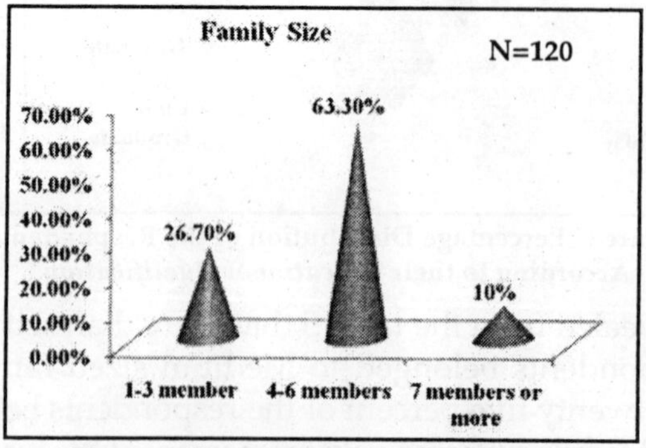


**Figure 8: Percentage Distribution of the Respondents According to their *Family Size***

**Table 6**
**Percentage Distribution of the Respondents According to their *Marital Status***

*N=120*

| *Marital Status* | *Frequency* | *Percentages (%)* |
|---|---|---|
| Single | 37 | 30.8 |
| Married | 78 | 65 |
| Widow | 4 | 3.3 |
| Separated | 1 | 0.83 |

Table 7 shows that very high majority eighty percent of the respondents had 1-2 children; seven percent of the respondents had no child whereas less tan five percent of the respondents had 3 or more children.

**Table 7**
**Percentage Distribution of the Respondents According to their Number of Children**

*N=83*

| *Number of Children* | *Frequency* | *Percentages (%)* |
|---|---|---|
| None | 6 | 7.2 |
| 1-2 children | 74 | 89.2 |
| 3 or more children | 3 | 3.6 |

It is revealed from the Table 8 that more than sixty percent of the respondents had less income per month whereas nearly forty percent of the respondents had more income per month.

**Table 8**
**Percentage Distribution of the Respondents According to their *Monthly Income***

*N= 120*

| *Monthly Income* | *Frequency* | *Percentages (%)* |
|---|---|---|
| Upto Rs. 10, 000 | 76 | 63.3 |
| More than Rs. 10, 000 | 44 | 36.7 |

Table 9 reveals that little less than seventy percent of the respondents had less earning members in the family whereas little more than thirty percent of the respondents had more earning members in the family.

**Table 9**
**Percentage Distribution of the Respondents According to the *Number of Earning Members in the Family***

N= 120

| *Number of Earning Members in the Family* | *Frequency* | *Percentages (%)* |
|---|---|---|
| Up to 2 members | 83 | 69.2 |
| 3 or more members | 37 | 30.8 |

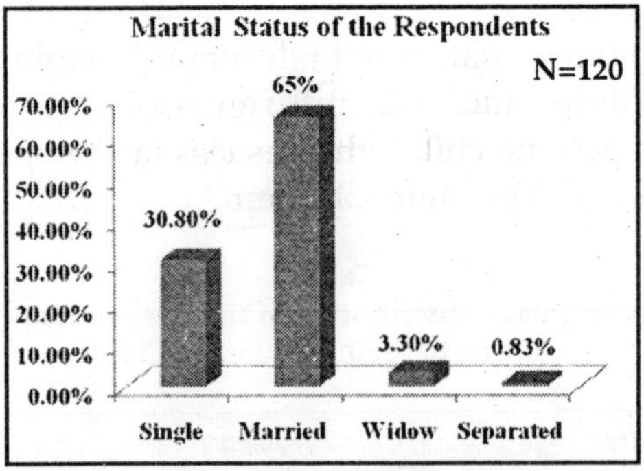


**Figure 9: Percentage Distribution of the Respondents According to their *Marital Status***

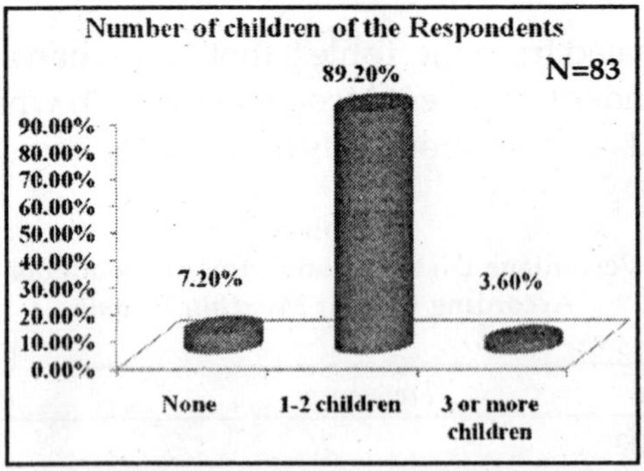


**Figure 10: Percentage Distribution of the Respondents According to their *Number of Children***

Table 10 shows that forty six percent of the respondents had less family income per month whereas fifty three percent of the respondents had more family income per month.

**Table 10**
**Percentage Distribution of the Respondents According to their *Family Income Per Month***

*N=120*

| *Family Income Per Month* | *Frequency* | *Percentages (%)* |
|---|---|---|
| Below Rs. 19, 000 | 56 | 46.7 |
| Above Rs. 19, 000 | 64 | 53.3 |

It can be seen from the Table 11 that forty nine percent of the respondents had Supportive response, thirty eight percent of the respondents had Co-operative response, fifteen percent of the respondents had Helpful response whereas very few three percent of the respondents had other type of response from the family.

**Table 11**
**Percentage Distribution of the Respondents According to Family Response**

*N=120*

| *Family Response* | *Frequency* | *Percentages (%)* |
|---|---|---|
| Supportive | 59 | 49.2 |
| Cooperative | 46 | 38.3 |
| Helpful | 21 | 17.5 |
| Any other | 4 | 3.3 |

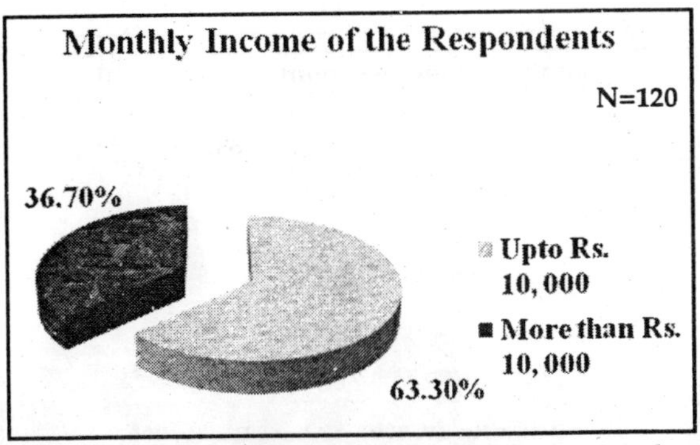


**Figure 11: Percentage Distribution of the Respondents According to their *Monthly Income***

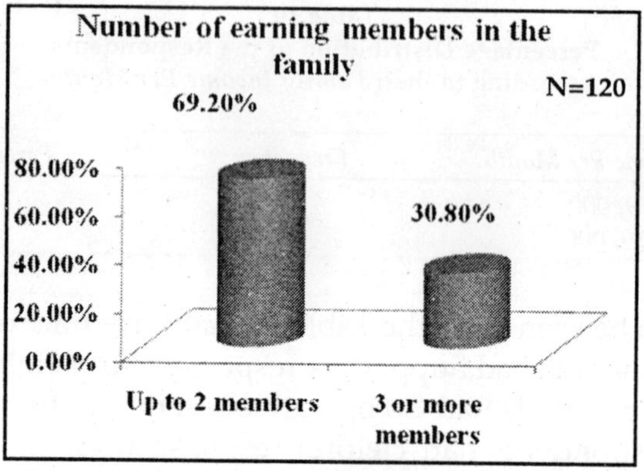


**Figure 12: Percentage Distribution of the Respondents According to the *Number of Earning Members in the Family***

Table 12 shows that high majority seventy five percent of the respondents had sufficient time to do household activities whereas thirty percent of the respondents did not get sufficient time to do household activities.

**Table 12**
**Percentage Distribution of the Respondents According to their *Sufficient Time to do Household Activities***

*N=120*

| *Get Sufficient Time to do Household Activities* | *Frequency* | *Percentages (%)* |
|---|---|---|
| Yes | 90 | 75 |
| No | 30 | 25 |

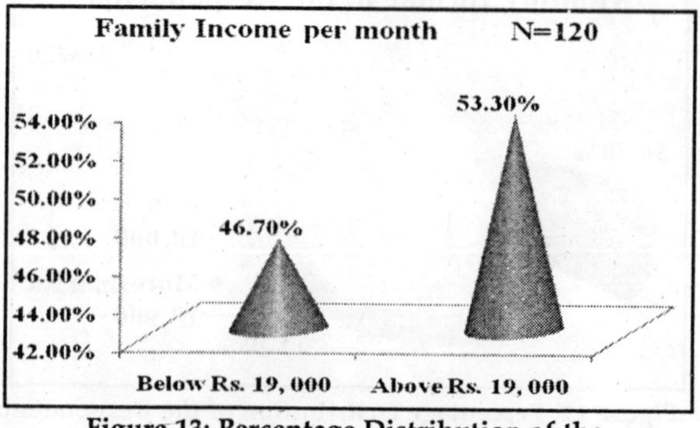


**Figure 13: Percentage Distribution of the Respondents According to *Family Income***

Table 13 shows that forty five percent of the respondents were doing cooking and Shopping by own selves, forty one percent of the respondents were doing cleaning, whereas ten percent of the respondents were doing other activities like helping children in their academic work, running tuition class, helping family members in other work like, go for paying bills, taxes, in bank work, mobile recharge etc.

**Table 13**
**Percentage Distribution of the Respondents According to their *Household Activities***

N= 120

| *Household Activities* | *Self (%)* | *Mother in Law (%)* | *Other Members of Family (%)* | *House Maid (%)* | *Any Other (%)* |
|---|---|---|---|---|---|
| Cooking | 45 | 6.7 | 17.5 | 6.7 | – |
| Cleaning | 40 | 4.2 | 19.2 | 25.8 | 1.7 |
| Shopping | 45.8 | 8.3 | 24.2 | 2.5 | 3.3 |
| Any other | 10.8 | 1.7 | 5 | 0.8 | 1.7 |

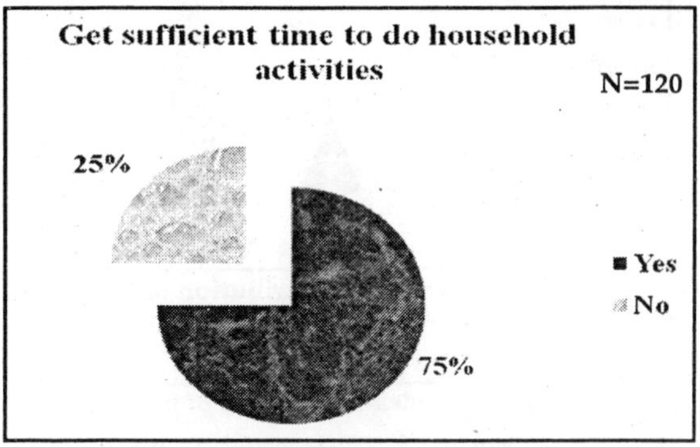


**Figure 14: Percentage Distribution of the Respondents According to their *Aufficient Time to do household Activities***

**Table 14**
**Percentage Distribution of the Respondents According to their *Job Designation***

*N= 120*

| *Job Designation* | *Frequency* | *Percentages (%)* |
|---|---|---|
| Class I | 29 | 24.2 |
| Class II | 20 | 16.7 |
| Class III | 71 | 59.2 |

It is revealed from the Table 14 that majority fifty nine percent of the respondents were from Class III, twenty four percent of the respondents were from Class I, few only sixteen percent of the respondents were from Class II.

**Table 15**
**Percentage Distribution of the Respondents According to their *Age at Starting of Job***

*N= 120*

| *Age of Respondents at Starting of Job* | *Frequency* | *Percentages (%)* |
|---|---|---|
| Upto 27 years | 96 | 80.0 |
| 28-33 years | 14 | 11.7 |
| 34 years and above | 10 | 8.3 |

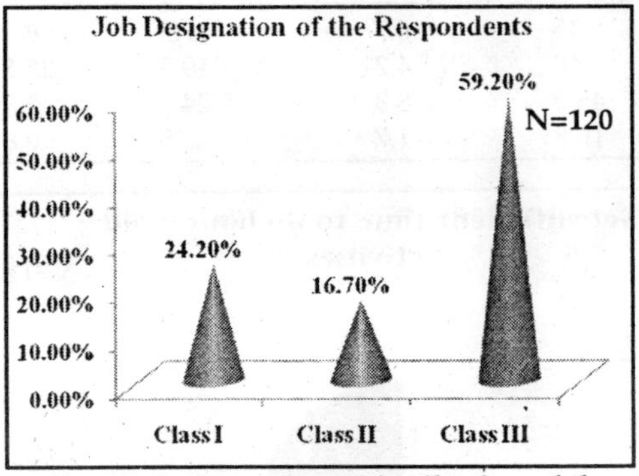


**Figure 15: Percentage Distribution of the Respondents According to their *Job Designation***

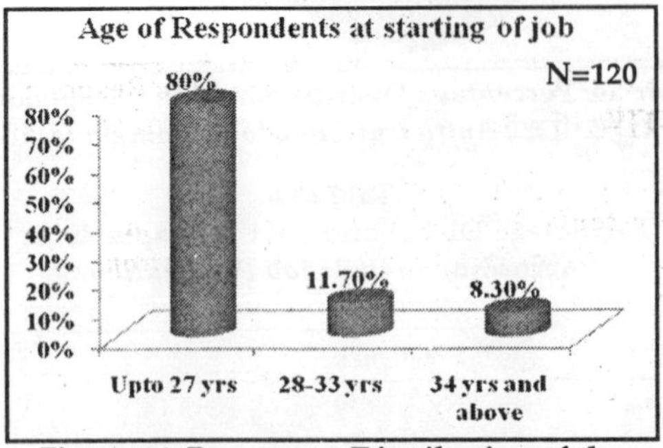


**Figure 16: Percentage Distribution of the Respondents According to their *Age at Starting of Job***

Table 15 reveals that high majority of eighty percent of the respondents had started their job at 27 years; little more than ten percent of the respondents had started their job between 28-33 years whereas less than ten percent of the respondents had started their job when they were 34 years and above.

Table 16 shows that majority fifty six percent of the respondents had to work for less hours, twenty five percent of the respondents had to work for few hours whereas seventeen percent of the respondents had to work for more hours.

**Table16**
**Percentage Distribution of the Respondents According to their *Working Hours***

*N= 120*

| *Working Hours* | *Frequency* | *Percentages (%)* |
|---|---|---|
| 3-5 hrs | 21 | 17.5 |
| 6-8 hrs | 68 | 56.7 |
| More than 8 hrs | 31 | 25.8 |

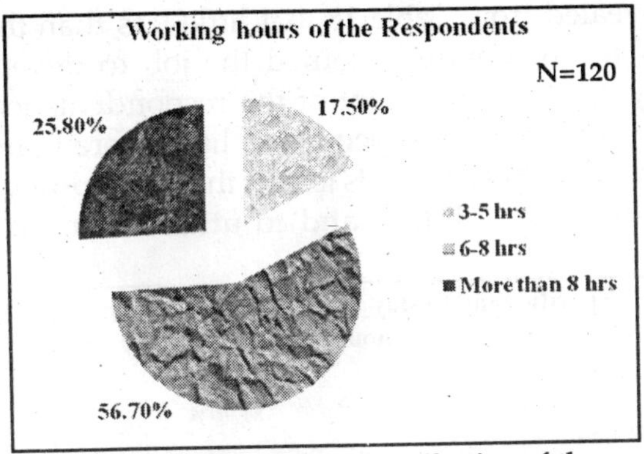


**Figure 16: Percentage Distribution of the Respondents According to their *Working Hours***

**Table 17**
**Percentage Distribution of the Respondents According to their Apecific Time to *Stay Back at Work for Long Hours***

*N= 120*

| *Specific Time to Stay Back at work for Long Hours* | *Frequency* | *Percentages (%)* |
|---|---|---|
| Yes | 58 | 48.3 |
| No | 62 | 51.7 |

Table 17 shows that fifty one percent of the respondents had no specific time to stay back at work for long hours where as forty eight percent of the respondents had specific time to stay back at work for long hours.

**Table 18**
**Percentage Distribution of the Respondents According to their *Reasons for Joining the Job***

*N= 120*

| *Reasons for Joining the Job* | *Frequency* | *Percentage (%)* |
|---|---|---|
| To supplement family income | 29 | 24.2 |
| To attain economic independence | 38 | 31.7 |
| To raise the standard of living of the family | 26 | 21.7 |
| To provide better education to children | 31 | 25.8 |
| To develop own personality | 39 | 32.5 |
| To keep oneself busy | 28 | 23.3 |
| To utilize one's education | 31 | 25.8 |
| Any other | 1 | 0.8 |

It is revealed from Table 18 that little less than thirty five percent of the respondents joined the job to develop own personality, thirty one percent of the respondents joined the job to attain economic independence, little more than twenty five percent of the respondents joined the job to provide better education to their children and to utilize own education,

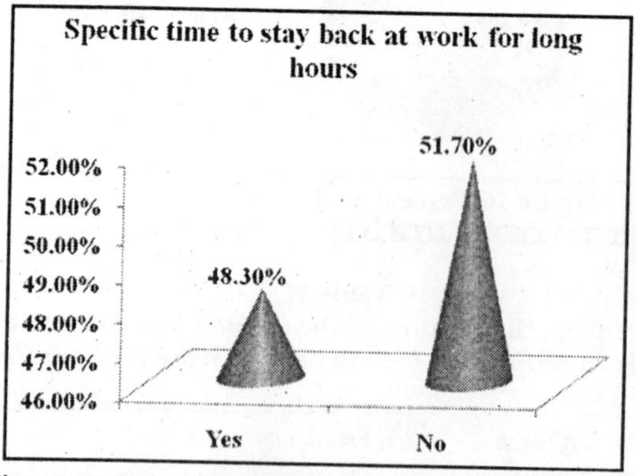


**Figure 17: Percentage Distribution of the Respondents According to their Specific Time to *Stay Back at Work for Long Hours***

twenty four percent of the respondents joined the job to supplement family income, whereas twenty one percent of the respondents joined the job to raise the standard of living of their family and only one percent of the respondents joined the job for other reasons.

**Table 19**
**Percentage Distribution of the Respondents According to their *Work Anywhere Else Before Taking up the Present Job***

*N= 120*

| *Work Anywhere Else before Taking up the Present Job* | *Frequency* | *Percentages (%)* |
|---|---|---|
| Yes | 60 | 50 |
| No | 60 | 50 |

The Table 19 shows that fifty percentage of the respondents had worked anywhere else before taking up the present job whereas fifty percent of the respondents had not worked anywhere else before taking up the present job.

**Table 20**
**Percentage Distribution of the Respondents According to their *Reasons for Changing the Earlier Job***

*N= 120*

| *Reasons for Changing the Earlier Job* | *Frequency* | *Percentages (%)* |
|---|---|---|
| Due to less salary | 25 | 41.7 |
| Due to poor work environment | 8 | 13.3 |
| The workplace was far from the house | 17 | 28.3 |
| Unpleasant atmosphere at workplace | 4 | 6.7 |
| Transfer of father/husband | 5 | 8.3 |
| Any other | 11 | 18.3 |

Table 20 reveals that forty one percent of the respondents changed the earlier job due to less salary, twenty eight percent of the respondents changed the earlier job due to the workplace was far from the house, little less than twenty percent of the respondents changed the earlier job due to other reasons, little less than fifteen percent of the respondents changed the earlier job due to poor work environment, and very few only eight percent of the respondents changed the earlier job due to transfer of father/ husband.

**Table 21**
**Percentage Distribution of the Respondents According to the *Reasons for Selecting the Present Job***

*N= 120*

| *Reasons for Selecting the Present Job* | *Frequency* | *Percentages (%)* |
|---|---|---|
| For better prospects in career | 55 | 45.8 |
| For better salary | 22 | 18.3 |
| For having interest in doing job | 39 | 32.5 |
| Workplace being near to the house | 15 | 12.5 |
| Any other | 10 | 8.3 |

Table 21 shows that forty five percent of the respondents selected the preset job for better prospects in the career, thirty two percent of the respondents selected the present job for having interest in doing job, whereas little less than twenty percent of the respondents selected the present job for better salary and very few twelve percent and eight percent of the respondents selected the present job for workplace being near to the house and for other reasons respectively.

**Table 22**
**Percentage Distribution of the Respondents According to their *Sources of Getting the Present Job***

*N= 120*

| *Sources of Getting the Present Job* | *Frequency* | *Percentages (%)* |
|---|---|---|
| Campus Recruitment | 6 | 5.0 |
| Friends | 25 | 20.8 |
| Family members and Relatives | 32 | 26.7 |
| Employment Exchange | 7 | 5.8 |
| Advertisements | 48 | 40.0 |
| Any other | 6 | 5 |

Table 22 reveals that forty percent of the respondents got this job through Advertisements, twenty six percent of the respondents got this job through family members and relatives, twenty percent of the respondents got this job through friends whereas very few only five percent of the respondents got this job through Campus Recruitment, Employment Exchange and through any other source respectively.

**Table 23**
**Percentage Distribution of the Respondents According to their *Facilities/ Benefits get from the Management***

N= 120

| *Facilities/ Benefits get from the Management* | *Frequency* | *Percentages (%)* |
|---|---|---|
| Canteen | 57 | 47.5 |
| Separate toilets for women | 74 | 61.7 |
| Separate rest rooms | 10 | 8.3 |
| Maternity Care/ Leave | 43 | 35.8 |
| Crèches | 5 | 4.2 |
| Medical Care | 27 | 22.5 |
| Any other | 13 | 10.8 |

It is revealed from Table 23 that majority sixty one percent of the respondents got Separate toilets facilities for women, forty seven percent of the respondents got Canteen facilities, thirty five percent of the respondents got Maternity Care/ Leave facilities, twenty two percent of the respondents got Medical Care facilities, whereas very few only eight percent of the respondents got Separate rest rooms and Crèches facilities from their Management.

**Table 24**
**Percentage Distribution of the Respondents According to their *Satisfaction with the Present Job***

N= 120

| *Satisfaction with the Present Job* | *Frequency* | *Percentages (%)* |
|---|---|---|
| Yes | 108 | 90 |
| No | 12 | 10 |

Table 24 shows that high majority ninety percent of the respondents were satisfied with their job whereas very few ten percent of the respondents were not satisfied with their job.

**Table 25**
**Percentage Distribution of the Respondents According to their *Reasons for Satisfaction with their Job***

*N= 120*

| *Reasons for Satisfaction* | *Frequency* | *Percentages (%)* |
|---|---|---|
| Because of good Salary | 29 | 24.2 |
| Because of good Work Environment | 50 | 41.7 |
| Due to workplace nearer to the house | 22 | 18.3 |
| Due to job as per choice | 43 | 35.8 |
| Any other | 2 | 1.67 |

Table 25 reveals that majority forty one percent of the respondents were satisfied because of good work environment, majority thirty five percent of the respondents were satisfied due to job as per choice, little less than twenty five percent of the respondents were satisfied with their job because of getting good salary, whereas only one percent of the respondents were satisfied because of other reason.

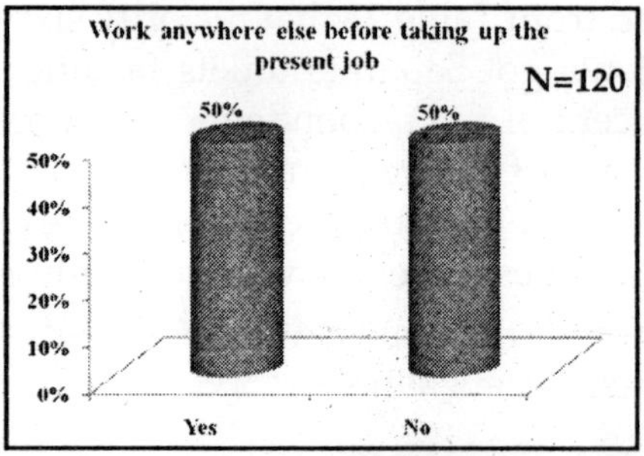


**Figure 18: Percentage Distribution of the Respondents According to their *Work Anywhere else before taking up the Present Job***

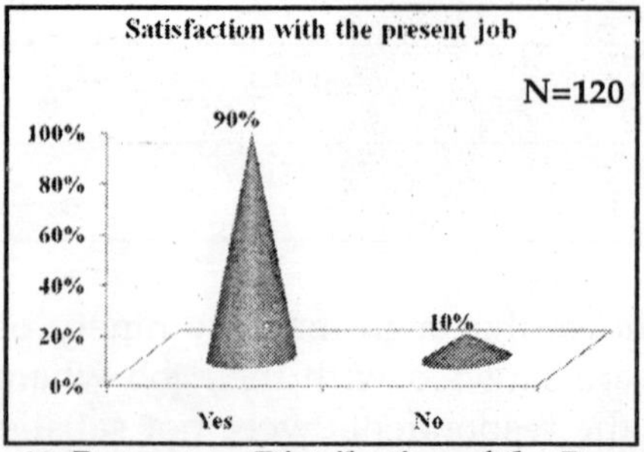


**Figure 19: Percentage Distribution of the Respondents According to their *Satisfaction with the Present Job***

**Table 26**
**Percentage Distribution of the Respondents According to having Independent Office**

*N= 120*

| *Respondents have Independent Office* | *Frequency* | *Percentages (%)* |
|---|---|---|
| Yes | 35 | 29.2 |
| No | 85 | 70.8 |

Table 26 shows that high majority seventy percent of the respondents have independent office in their organization whereas little less than thirty five percent of the respondents have not independent office in their organization.

**Table 27**
**Percentage Distribution of the Respondents According to their *Adequate Furniture Available in the Office***

*N= 120*

| *Adequate Furniture Available in the Office* | *Frequency* | *Percentages (%)* |
|---|---|---|
| Yes | 32 | 91.4 |
| No | 3 | 8.6 |

Table 27 shows that high majority ninety one percent of the respondents had Adequate furniture available in their office whereas very few eight percent of the respondents reported that they do not have Adequate furniture available in their office.

**Table 28**
**Percentage Distribution of the Respondents According to their *Category of their Job***

*N= 120*

| *Category of their Job* | *Frequency* | *Percentages (%)* |
|---|---|---|
| Skilled | 91 | 75.8 |
| Semi Skilled | 26 | 21.7 |
| Unskilled | 3 | 2.5 |

It is revealed from Table 28 that high majority of seventy five percent of the respondents had skilled job, twenty one percent of the respondents had Semi-skilled job whereas only two percent of the respondents had unskilled job.

Table 29 reveals that fifty percent of the respondents reported friendly and cooperative behavior, where as thirty two percent of the respondents got Supportive behavior and twenty eight percent of the respondents got Understandable behavior whereas little more than fifteen percent of the respondents got Courteous behavior from their colleagues.

**Table 29**
**Percentage Distribution of the Respondents According to Type of *Behavior they get from their Colleagues***

*N= 120*

| *Type of behavior they get from their Colleagues* | *Frequency* | *Percentages (%)* |
|---|---|---|
| Understanding | 34 | 28.3 |
| Supportive | 39 | 32.5 |
| Courteous | 20 | 16.7 |
| Friendly | 60 | 50 |
| Co-operative | 60 | 50 |
| Humiliating | 4 | 3.3 |
| Any other | – | – |

Table 30 shows that high majority ninety percent of the respondents found their workplace comfortable enough to meet their job demands whereas very few only ten percent of the respondents did not find their workplace comfortable enough to meet their job demands.

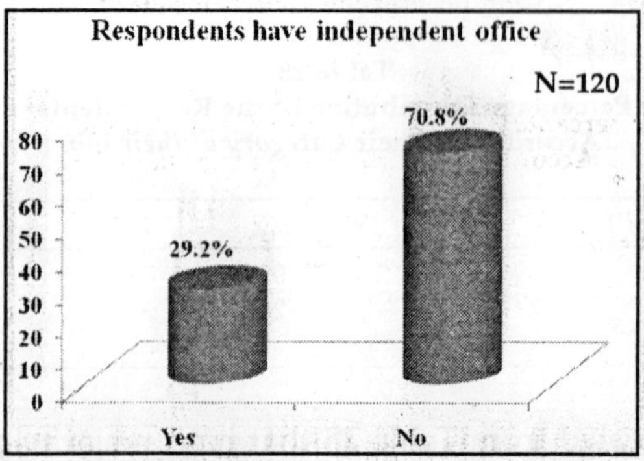


**Figure 20: Percentage Distribution of the Respondents According to *having Independent Office***

**Table 30**
**Percentage Distribution of the Respondents According to Finding *Workplace Comfortable Enough to Meet their Job Demands***

*N= 120*

| *Finding Workplace Comfortable enough to meet their Job Demands* | *Frequency* | *Percentages (%)* |
|---|---|---|
| Yes | 108 | 90 |
| No | 12 | 10 |

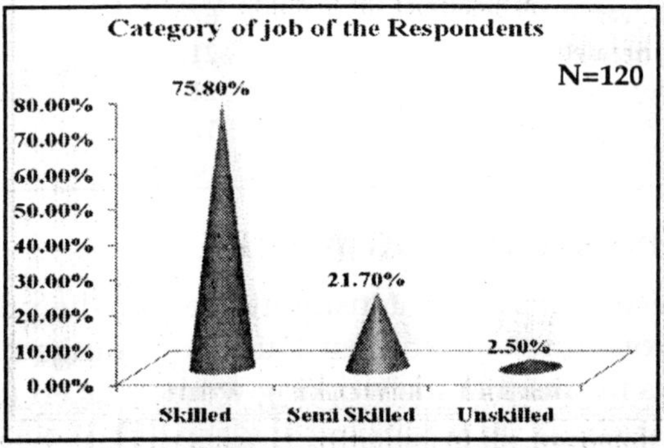


**Figure 21: Percentage Distribution of the Respondents According to their *Category of their Job***

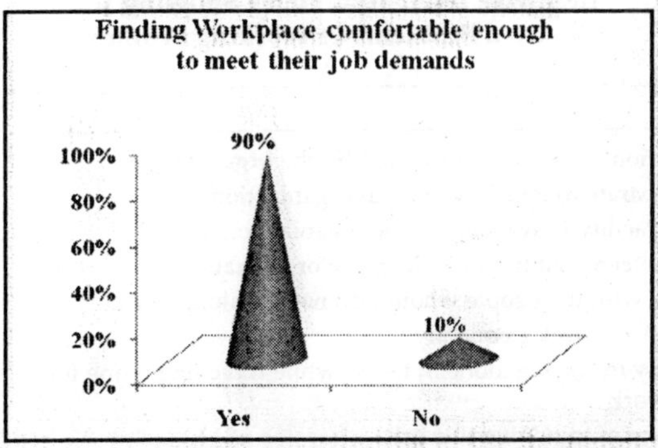


**Figure 22: Percentage Distribution of the Respondents According to Finding *Workplace Comfortable Enough to meet their Job Demands***

Table 31 shows that majority fifty five percent of the respondents used Personal Conveyance, whereas seventeen percent of the respondents used Conveyance provided by the office and public transport to reach their office, whereas very few only ten percent of the respondents reached their office by walking and very few one percent of the respondents reached their office by railway.

**Table 31**
**Percentage Distribution of the Respondents According to their *Mode of Transport Used to reach Office***

*N= 120*

| *Mode of Transport used to reach Office* | *Frequency* | *Percentages (%)* |
|---|---|---|
| Personal Conveyance | 67 | 55.8 |
| Conveyance provided by Office | 21 | 17.5 |
| Public Transport | 21 | 17.5 |
| By walking | 12 | 10 |
| Any other (Railway) | 2 | 1.7 |

## PROBLEMS OF WORKING WOMEN

Table 32 reveals that the intensity indices for the problems of working women related to their Paid work ranged from 1.65 to 1.08. This means that the working women faced Job related problems.

**Table 32**
**Itemwise Intensity Indices Showing Job Related Problems of Working Women**

*N=120*

| *Problems* | *I.I* |
|---|---|
| No transportation services are provided by the organization. | 1.65 |
| There is no separate toilet for women in organization. | 1.33 |
| No rest room facility is available in the organization. | 1.60 |
| There is no canteen facility available in the organization. | 1.43 |
| I have to work with the people whom I do not get along with. | 1.37 |
| I have to travel for work frequently. | 1.08 |
| I have difficulty in staying alone in hotels while travelling alone for professional work. | 1.14 |
| I don't get peace of mind due to work. | 1.19 |
| My job demands extra hours of work. | 1.28 |
| I get tired due to work. | 1.38 |
| I am overloaded with the work which is greater than that of the other colleagues. | 1.26 |
| My pay is not adequate to fulfill my financial needs. | 1.27 |
| I do not get promotion in the job. | 1.39 |
| I do not get adequate powers to perform my job in a better manner. | 1.30 |

*Contd.*

| *Problems* | *I.I* |
|---|---|
| I do not get fair treatment from my colleagues. | 1.17 |
| I am unable to concentrate on the work due to some of the peculiar habits of my co-workers like too much of interference in my work. | 1.17 |
| I do not get help from other colleagues. | 1.18 |
| My colleagues dominate me. | 1.15 |
| There is internal jealously among the staff members, which hamper the professional growth. | 1.31 |
| There is negative propaganda by male staff which is harming the professional status and personal life. | 1.15 |
| My superiors do not consider my personal genuine problems. | 1.27 |
| My authorities indicate favourism/bias towards other employees. | 1.32 |
| My job does not give me enough experiences, which leads to dissatisfaction. | 1.16 |
| I find lack of opportunity for advancement in the job attending training programmes. | 1.32 |
| I do not get time to attend seminars/workshops/lectures for professional growth. | 1.35 |
| My suggestions are not accepted by subordinates like in official matters or in organizing any official programmes. | 1.16 |
| I have sleep disturbances due to job stress. | 1.26 |
| My job demands extra hours of work. | 1.28 |
| I get tired due to work. | 1.12 |
| I am overloaded with the work which is greater than that of the other colleagues. | 1.22 |
| My pay is not adequate to fulfill my financial needs. | 1.09 |
| I do not get promotion in the job. | 1.28 |
| I do not get adequate powers to perform my job in a better manner. | 1.23 |
| I am not happy with the commute between work and home. | 1.27 |
| I feel that my life is usually filled with deadlines. | 1.26 |

The items on Paid work related problems like, No transportation services; No rest room facility; No canteen facility available in the organization; No rest room facility is available in the organization, Do not get promotion in the job were the problems which the respondents faced more at their workplaces. The items on Paid work related to problems like, Have to travel for work frequently; Pay is not adequate to fulfill financial needs; get tired due to work; Have difficulty in staying alone in hotels while travelling alone for professional work and Negative propaganda by male staff which is harming the professional status and personal life were the problems which the respondents faced to a less extent at their workplaces.

**Table 33**
**Itemwise Intensity Indices Showing Household Work Related Problems of Working Women**

*N=120*

| *Problems* | *I.I* |
|---|---|
| I have difficulty in carrying out family responsibilities like unable to cope up with the work at home. | 1.38 |
| I am overburdened at home like taking care of sick/elderly family members. | 1.21 |
| I am unable to spend peaceful time with family members during holidays. | 1.27 |
| I am unable to work according to the expectation of my family members like going out for vacations, cooking their favourite meal etc. | 1.36 |
| I am unable to attend relatives/ guests at home. | 1.39 |
| I do not get cooperation from my family members in sharing household responsibilities. | 1.12 |
| I lack confidence in housekeeping tasks. | 1.15 |
| I do not find reliable servant which creates difficulty in managing household work. | 1.24 |
| My servant remains absent in the peak hours of work. | 1.2 |
| My servant is not efficient. | 1.15 |
| I cannot afford a servant. | 1.07 |
| I am unable to attend social functions like marriage ceremonies and other functions. | 1.38 |
| I have to fulfill too many social expectations/ obligations. | 1.29 |
| I do not get cooperation from my husband. | 1.08 |
| My husband is not satisfied with my household work. | 1.19 |
| I am neglected from my husband. | 1.05 |
| My in laws complaint to my husband regarding my household work. | 1.13 |
| I am unable to fulfill my hobbies like knitting, reading, painting etc. due to lack of time. | 1.51 |
| My children are too small and I cannot leave them alone. | 1.23 |
| There is non-availability of day care centers/ pre-nursery/play centers near home/workplace. | 1.20 |
| I am unable to give full attention to the needs of my children. | 1.41 |
| I am unable to help my children in doing their academic work. | 0.71 |
| My children perform below expectations due to lack of guidance by me. | 1.24 |
| My children suffer in studies as they have to do household work. | 1.14 |
| There is a lack of children's park nearby. | 1.15 |
| Conflicts take place between my husband and me pertaining to children. | 1.20 |
| Disputes take place between my family members and me pertaining to household duties. | 1.17 |
| I do not get any preferential treatment in the family on account of | 1.12 |

*Contd.*

| *Problems* | *I.I* |
|---|---|
| being working women like not giving consideration to my opinion in family decisions. | |
| I face opposition of family members for my job. | 1.11 |
| I never handled any responsibility as I was over protected. | 1.12 |
| I have lack of time due to overburden of housekeeping activities. | 1.38 |
| I am unable to help my husband for such activities like go to pay Telephone and Mobile bills, Electricity bills, different Taxes etc. | 1.56 |
| I am unable to adjust myself with the changing life. | 1.13 |
| I have less interest in doing household activities. | 1.16 |
| I have to suffer due to expectations of family members for hot meal food. | 1.37 |

Table 33 reveals that the intensity indices for the problems of working women related to their Household work ranged from 1.56 to 0.71. This means that the working women faced Household work related problems.

The items on Household work related problems like, Unable to help husband for such activities like go to pay Telephone and Mobile bills, Electricity bills, different Taxes etc; Unable to fulfill hobbies like knitting, reading, painting etc. due to lack of time; unable to give full attention to the needs of my children; Unable to attend relatives/guests at home and Unable to attend social functions like marriage ceremonies and other functions were the problems which the respondents faced more in their Household work. The items on Household work related problems like, facing opposition of family members for their job; Do not get cooperation from husband, Cannot afford a servant; Neglect from husband and Unable to help children in doing their academic work were the problems which the respondents faced less in their Household work.

## DIFFERENCES IN THE PROBLEMS OF WORKING WOMEN

Overall Differences, Differences in the Job related problems and Differences in the Household work related problems of working women can be shown in Appendix III.

**Table 34**
**Overall Differences in the Problems of Working Women**

*N=120*

*ANOVA*

| *Source of Variance* | *Sum of Squares* | *Df* | *Mean Square* | *F* | *Sig.* |
|---|---|---|---|---|---|
| **Age** | | | | | |
| Between Groups | 3172.415 | 2 | 1586.208 | 10.641 | .000* |
| Within Groups | 17440.510 | 117 | 149.064 | | |
| Total | 20612.925 | 119 | | | |
| **Type of family** | | | | | |
| Between Groups | 76.732 | 2 | 38.366 | .219 | .804 |
| Within Groups | 20536.193 | 117 | 175.523 | | |
| Total | 20612.925 | 119 | | | |
| **Experience** | | | | | |
| Between Groups | 912.366 | 2 | 456.183 | 2.709 | .071 |
| Within Groups | 19700.559 | 117 | 168.381 | | |
| Total | 20612.925 | 119 | | | |
| **Distance from workplace** | | | | | |
| Between Groups | 296.924 | 2 | 148.462 | .855 | .428 |
| Within Groups | 20316.001 | 117 | 173.641 | | |
| Total | 20612.925 | 119 | | | |

* Significant at 0.05 level

There were *significant differences* in the overall problems of working women in relation to their *Age* and *no significant differences* in the overall problems of working women in relation to their *Type of family, Experience* and *Distance from the workplace.*

**Table 35**
**Differences in the Job Related Problems of Working Women**

*N=120*

*ANOVA*

| *Source of Variance* | *Sum of Squares* | *Df* | *Mean Square* | *F* | *Sig.* |
|---|---|---|---|---|---|
| **Age** | | | | | |
| Between Groups | 29.119 | 2 | 14.560 | .328 | .721 |
| Within Groups | 5198.206 | 117 | 44.429 | | |
| Total | 5227.325 | 119 | | | |
| **Type of family** | | | | | |
| Between Groups | 114.984 | 2 | 57.492 | 1.316 | .272 |

*Contd.*

| *ANOVA* | | | | | |
|---|---|---|---|---|---|
| *Source of Variance* | *Sum of Squares* | *Df* | *Mean Square* | *F* | *Sig.* |
| Within Groups | 5112.341 | 117 | 43.695 | | |
| Total | 5227.325 | 119 | | | |
| **Experience** | | | | | |
| Between Groups | 42.656 | 2 | 21.328 | .481 | .619 |
| Within Groups | 5184.669 | 117 | 44.313 | | |
| Total | 5227.325 | 119 | | | |
| **Distance from workplace** | | | | | |
| Between Groups | 1.306 | 2 | 653 | .015 | .985 |
| Within Groups | 5226.019 | 117 | 44.667 | | |
| Total | 5227.325 | 119 | | | |

There were *no significant differences* in the problems of working women related to their Paid work in relation to their *Age, Type of family, Experience* and *Distance from the workplace.*

**Table 36**
**Differences in the Household Work Problems of Working Women**

*N=120*

| *Source of Variance* | *Sum of Squares* | *Df* | *Mean Square* | *F* | *Sig.* |
|---|---|---|---|---|---|
| **Age** | | | | | |
| Between Groups | 3253.256 | 2 | 1626.628 | 27.236 | .000* |
| Within Groups | 6987.544 | 117 | 59.723 | | |
| Total | 10240.800 | 119 | | | |
| **Type of family** | | | | | |
| Between Groups | 141.518 | 2 | 70.759 | .820 | .443 |
| Within Groups | 10099.282 | 117 | 86.319 | | |
| Total | 10240.800 | 119 | | | |
| **Experience** | | | | | |
| Between Groups | 1343.602 | 2 | 671.801 | 8.834 | .000* |
| Within Groups | 8897.198 | 117 | 76.044 | | |
| Total | 10240.800 | 119 | | | |
| **Distance from workplace** | | | | | |
| Between Groups | 314.735 | 2 | 157.368 | 1.855 | .161 |
| Within Groups | 9926.065 | 117 | 84.838 | | |
| Total | 10240.800 | 119 | | | |

* Significant at 0.05 level

There were *Significant differences* in the problems of working women related to their Household work in relation to their *Age* and *Experience* and there were *no significant differences* in the problems of working women related to their Household work in relation to their *Type of family* and *Distance from workplace*.

## *COPING UP STRATEGIES USED BY WORKING WOMEN TO MANAGE STRESS*

Table 37 reveals that the intensity indices for the problems of working women related to their Household work ranged from 3.52 to 1.72. This means that the working women faced problems ranged from more to less problems related to their Household work.

**Table 37**
**Percentage Distribution of the Respondents According to Coping up Strategies Used by them to Manage Stress**

*N=120*

| *Coping up Strategies to manage stress* | *I.I* |
|---|---|
| *When I am under stress I try to cope with the situation using the following:* | |
| I exercise. | 2.59 |
| I include regular breathing exercises. | 2.72 |
| I practice meditation. | 2.78 |
| I smoke. | 3.7 |
| I take more fried and heavy food. | 3.34 |
| I increase my caffeine intake (Coffee, Tea, and Cola). | 3.04 |
| I compulsively work. | 3.09 |
| I set myself unrealistic goals. | 2.47 |
| I blame other people. | 3.32 |
| I plan ahead for events that may be potentially stressful. | 2.87 |
| I organize my time to do things that are important to me. | 3.3 |
| I can make decisions without undue anxiety. | 1.72 |
| I try to help others. | 3.21 |
| I take enough breaks to reduce the monotonous nature of my work. | 2.96 |
| I try to control the situation around me. | 3.22 |
| I try to change situations. | 2.01 |
| I take situations as an opportunity to learn. | 3.3 |
| I try to change my priorities. | 2.13 |
| I compromise to get something positive out of the situation. | 3.25 |
| I console myself with the hope that things will get better. | 3.28 |

*Contd.*

| *Coping up Strategies to manage stress* | *I.I* |
|---|---|
| *When I am under stress I try to cope with the situation using the following:* | |
| I try to get out of the situation gracefully. | 1.9 |
| I physically withdraw myself from the situation. | 2.9 |
| I postpone decisions pertaining to the problem. | 2.79 |
| I give the situation extra attention. | 3.02 |
| I often try to use humor to diffuse tension. | 2.87 |
| I include some relaxation time in my daily routine. | 3.16 |
| I try and enjoy moments of pleasure. | 3.35 |
| I maintain good relationships with others, especially those closest to me. | 3.52 |
| I have someone with whom I discuss personal worries or problems. | 3.15 |
| I express what I feel or believe without feeling anxious. | 3.17 |
| I deny that there is a problem. | 2.72 |

The items on Coping up Strategies like, Maintain good relationships with others, especially those closest to me; Try and enjoy moments of pleasure; Organize the time to do things that are important to women; Take situations as an opportunity to learn; Console with the hope that things will get better; Try to control the situation around them; Practice meditation and Can make decisions without undue anxiety were the coping up strategies strongly agreed and agreed by the respondents. The items on Coping up strategies like, Try to get out of the situation gracefully; Try to change situations; Set oneself unrealistic goals; Deny that there is a problem; Postpone decisions pertaining to the problem; Blame other people; Take more fried and heavy food and Smoke were the coping up strategies disagreed and strongly disagreed by the respondents.

## SUGGESTIONS TO REDUCE THE PROBLEMS OF WORKING WOMEN

The items on Suggestions like in each organization, separate toilet facility for women should be compulsory; the rule should be strongly implemented to stop women's harassment at workplace by the organization; increasing positive attitude towards working women, increase the awareness in the society; Women should be made aware of their constitutional and legal rights by Educational Institutions; The rule for providing enough salary to working women should be strongly implemented; Give substantial allowances to women for their medical expenses; Give vocational training to women to increase their efficiency; Maternity benefit schemes should be enhanced by the Government; Women should be trained to develop their capabilities of decision making; Burden of household work of working women should be reduced were the suggestions which the respondents suggested to a great extent

**Table 38**
**Percentage Distribution of the Respondents According to the Suggestions to Reduce their Problems**

*N=120*

| *Suggestions to Reduce the Problems of Working Women* | *I.I.* |
|---|---|
| Canteen facility should be provided by the organization. | 2.65 |
| Rest room facility should be provided by the organization for reducing tired during the recess time. | 2.37 |
| In each organization, Separate toilet facility for women should be compulsory. | 2.92 |
| Every sector should have a transportation service of its own. | 2.32 |
| Strengthening of childcare facilities near the working place by the institutions. | 2.43 |
| The entertaining programmes should be usually organized by the organization. | 2.35 |
| Indoor games should be usually arranged by the organization. | 2.21 |
| In house journals should be published regularly in the organization so that the women can present their own thoughts. | 2.44 |
| Special functions should be organized in the organization like welcome to new employee, employee's leave or celebration of her birthday etc. | 2.62 |
| Women should be given vocational training to increase their efficiency. | 2.69 |
| Women should be trained to develop their capabilities of decision making. | 2.67 |
| Women should be made aware of their constitutional and legal rights by Educational Institutions. | 2.79 |
| Maternity benefit schemes should be enhanced by the Government. | 2.69 |

*Contd.*

| *Suggestions to Reduce the Problems of Working Women* | *I.I.* |
|---|---|
| The rule for providing enough salary to working women should be strongly implemented. | 2.77 |
| Women should be given substantial allowances for medical expenses. | 2.7 |
| To stop women's harassment at workplace, the rule should be strongly implemented by the organization. | 2.87 |
| More seminars, conferences and workshops should be organized for the working women. | 2.44 |
| Health services like health check-ups, yoga/ exercise should be organized time to time by the institution. | 2.5 |
| The organization should provide family welfare services and professional counseling services. | 2.46 |
| Working Women's Association should be formed. | 2.22 |
| Husband should come forward to share responsibilities. | 2.5 |
| Burden of household work of working women should be reduced. | 2.63 |
| To increase positive attitude towards working women, the awareness should be increased in the society. | 2.83 |

Table 38 reveals that the intensity indices for the problems of working women related to their Household work ranged from 2.92 to 2.63. This means that the working women faced problems related to their Household work from less intensity to more intensity.

The items on Suggestions like in each organization, separate toilet facility for women should be compulsory; the rule should be strongly implemented to stop women's harassment at workplace by the organization; increasing positive attitude towards working women, increase the awareness in the society; Women should be made aware of their constitutional and legal rights by Educational Institutions; The rule for providing enough salary to working women should be strongly implemented; Give substantial allowances to women for their medical expenses; Give vocational training to women to increase their efficiency; Maternity benefit schemes should be enhanced by the Government; Women should be trained to develop their capabilities of decision making; Burden of household work of working women should be reduced were the suggestions which the respondents suggested to a great extent.

# 5

# DISCUSSION

This chapter presents discussion related to the findings of the study and its implications.

## BACKGROUND INFORMATION

The total number of respondents who responded to the questionnaire were 120 women. The findings revealed that majority of the respondents belonged to nuclear family. A small percentage of respondents belonged to joint and extended family. Hence, for majority their family size would also be small in comparison to the size of the joint and extended family. This is the common picture of urbanization and modernization where working women are involved in white collar as well as blue collar jobs in urban areas. Thus, it is possible that they may be enjoying more freedom and flexibility in terms of familial responsibilities thereby, reducing their problems. This was supported by the findings of the researcher Rath (1987) that the employed women living in nuclear families had better adjusted married life than those living in joint families. This was also supported by the findings of the researcher Christopher (2001) that more than half of the respondents live in nuclear families which is highly preferred by married working women at present because of the individuality and freedom enjoyed by them in the same. This finding is supported by similar findings by Deshpande (1992) on the problems of working wives. It was found that most of the working women came from nuclear family because the nuclear family is free from most of the traditional restriction about female behavior and there is more freedom for women to seek employment.

The findings also revealed that majority of the respondents had 4-6 members in their family. The less percentage of the respondents had 1-6 members and 7 members or more in their family. This may be because of breakdown of joint family system due to urbanization.

The findings also revealed that from the married respondents, high majority of the respondents had 1-2 children. This may be because of increase in nuclear family system; the working mothers must have faced difficult situations in the upbringing of children. The findings of the present study also revealed that the respondents were from different occupations such as doctors, engineers, administrative officers, college teachers, school teachers, extension officers, NGO Workers, clerks, nurses, and executives.

The present study also revealed that majority of the respondents had 1-6 years of work experience. The reason may be that respondents were young and less experienced. The findings also revealed that majority of the respondents had 6-8 hours of work at their workplace. It may be inferred that the profession of engineers, officers had to stay at workplace for 6-8 hours and sometimes it could be more also.

The reasons given by the respondents for joining job in the present study was that they wanted to utilize their education and to provide better education to children. Working for providing better education to children as expressed by the respondents, throws light on their changing values regarding education. This shows that women have become conscious to utilize their educational qualifications in terms of taking up gainful employment. They have started giving importance to the education and its benefits for them as well as for the family's development.

It was also evident from the present study that majority of the women had educational qualification up to graduation. It reflects that the highly qualified women are inspired to go for career development by taking up gainful employment and thus, utilizing their education. This finding was supported by a similar finding by Wadhera (1976) revealed that professional and highly qualified women took up employment to utilize their education and training to the economic needs of their family. Whereas Kalia (1999) stated that, in India most of the women seek outside jobs to a great extent due to economic necessity. Whereas, today women are also taking up job to utilize their education in addition to fulfilling functions as wife and mother.

It was also found from the study that women joined employment to provide better education to their children. The probable reason may be that being highly qualified; she might have the strong feeling that education brings better status in society. So, this could also be possible through sending their children to a renowned school which would further offer them better facilities, education and status to their children in the future. The expenses of such school may be quite high which further compelled the women to earn by taking up the job in order to meet these expenses and provide better educational opportunities to their children.

Further, the findings of the present study revealed that majority of the respondents selected the present job for better prospects in career and for having interest in doing the job. The probable reason may be that the job provides better facility and security along with the fixed hours of work.

It is also evident from the present study that majority of the respondents who had been engaged previously with another job changed due to less salary and due to workplace which was far from the house. The reason may be that their previous job might not be offering better salary, which may not be able to fulfill their financial as well as the personal needs. Further, the findings of the present study revealed that high majority of the respondents had skilled job and found their workplace comfortable enough to meet their job demands. The reason may be that their job provided good training and skills about different types of works. It is also evident from the present study that majority of the respondents had upto 2 kms distance from their home to the workplace and mainly used personal conveyance to reach their workplace.

## JOB RELATED PROBLEMS OF WORKING WOMEN

It is evident from the study that majority of the respondents had more job related problems. The probable reason may be that the workplaces do not offer more security and respect. So, the working women had more problems because these workplaces do not offer good facilities which may not provide them job satisfaction and thus it indicates more problems.

The job related problems such as no transportation facility and no rest room facilities and no canteen facilities in their organization, did not get promotion in their job, got tired due to work; had to work with the people whom they did not get along well, did not get time to attend seminars/workshops/lectures for professional growth, lack of opportunity for advancement in the job attending training programmes and did not get adequate powers to perform their job in a better manner. The probable reason could be that the promotion criteria are fixed, where the experience of an employee is one criterion considered whilst promotion. It is also evident from the present study that majority of the working women had less experience. Therefore, they might not have received the promotion inspite of their efficient work.

Similar findings were reported by a study conducted by Kraisonswasdi (1989) that majority of the women executives in the public sector (89.32 percent) were of the opinion that an individual's ability is given a limited weightage in their organization at the time of promotion. The respondents clearly indicated that in the public sector promotion is determined by other considerations and qualifications where in most of the cases it is not the best qualified person who moves to the top.

The findings further revealed that the respondents do not get fair treatment from colleagues and do not get help from other colleagues. Banerji and Sen (2000) reported similar findings that the treatment of superiors towards women employees does not alone determine the status of women in office. As a women employed in an office has not only superiors but also colleagues and subordinates. They further reported that the respect earned from the colleagues can be measured on account of the aspects like cooperation from colleagues, appreciation of good work, recognition from colleagues, behavior expressing resentment and Being given all unpleasant work. The reason may be that the male colleagues and subordinates do not treat the women equally with other male staff members by giving respect and cooperation, the women would not be allowed to work as efficiently as she could.

## HOUSEHOLD WORK RELATED PROBLEMS OF WORKING WOMEN

There has been a positive change that the spouse have realized that domestic fulfillment could not be exclusive responsibility or concern of either one. Since, women have shared economic burden of the family and help to reduce the drudgery at home, now husbands have also come forward to share the domestic responsibilities on the household front. The women have shared economic burden of the family, thereby reducing the problems at home. The findings of the study revealed that the working women were unable to fulfill their hobbies like knitting, reading, painting etc., unable to help their husband for such activities like paying Telephone and Mobile bills, Electricity bills, different Taxes, unable to give full attention to the needs of their children due to lack of time, have to suffer due to expectations of family members for hot meal. The women devoted less time for training and caring of their children. They found less time to meet the demands of their family members such as serving the hot food to their family members. It implies that since these women are working, they are not able to give time for their children and family. Voluntary organizations and government organizations should organize educational and leisure time activities for their children nearer to their localities. This will take care of the children's time which otherwise would be spent unproductively and directionless. These children can utilize constructive time when their mothers are away.

As these women had small children, and many of the women did not get cooperation from in-laws and husbands, they had to perform many family responsibilities by themselves. That became a problem for them. Husbands of some respondents were posted in some other place and that was the cause of problems in performing household responsibilities alone. A small percentage of respondents did not get co-operation from their husbands also. Similar findings were reported by Agrawal (1988) that the husbands who were placed in a superior position did not co-operate with their wives as good as the husbands of same profession. The reasons may be that different working hours or different nature of job of husband was also the hindering factor to give much help to the wife even if both possessed equal status in job. Arya (1990) also reported that the working wife herself in confused and the attitude of her husband and society in ambivalent. The reason may be that the husband does not want his wife to be independent and only expect her to be obedient submissive wife. Thus working wife does not get cooperation from her husband. This thinking pattern has caused multiple socio-psychological problems. Again, it could be possible that in terms of their family life, the working women may still have to do several domestic chores and claim that they had no difficulty in this regard, inspite of their full time job. It is also possible that the help, which they receive from the other members of the family in doing chores, is really sufficient. Supporting this is Kalia (1999) in the research on psychological profile of the female executive in Mumbai city reported that family plays a key role in influencing the duties of a woman at home. Once the woman is able to attain the cooperation of the family, she overcomes a major hurdle.

The findings of the present study further revealed that the problems like had difficulty in carrying out family responsibilities like unable to cope up with the domestic work at home and were unable to attend relatives/ guests at home, social functions like marriage ceremonies and other functions. The probable reason could be that the most of the time of the working women was engaged in performing dual responsibilities. So, they may not get extra time for themselves to fulfill their hobbies and personal needs. Even it may also be possible that there weekly offs or evening time and other holidays are also spent on doing the pending household work, which the working women are not able to finish during working days. Family has always remained in the nucleus of the women's activities and therefore, whatever time was left with women, apart from daily activities; they would like to satisfy their family needs rather than fulfilling their own hobbies. Murty (2001) also found that majority of the working women feel that they are not able to pay enough attention to their household task and that their children are also not getting desired attention. Mukhopadhyay (1999) also found that dual roles in family and workplace often make a working woman more tense. It was also noted that role ambiguity, role conflict and the degree of responsibility were the main sources of stress among working women.

## COPING UP STRATEGIES USED BY WORKING WOMEN TO MANAGE STRESS

Work is an essential part of our lives. There are people who find real satisfaction in their work but there are people who get really stressed out because of their work situation. There are different factors that play a role with an individual suffering from stress in their job situation. Personal, interpersonal and organizational factors have been reported to relate to stress and burnout.

It was revealed from the present study that coping up strategies like maintain good relationships with others, especially those who are close, try and enjoy moments of pleasure, organize time to do things that are important to me, Take situations as an opportunity to learn were strongly agreed by the respondents. It means that when the respondents are under stress, they use these positive strategies to manage stress.

The coping up strategies like try to get out of the situation gracefully; try to change situations; set oneself unrealistic goals; deny that there is a problem; postpone decisions pertaining to the problem; blame other people; take more fried and heavy food and smoke were strongly disagreed by the respondents. It means that when the respondents are under stress, they do not use these negative strategies to manage stress.

The findings of the study revealed that majority of the respondents use coping up strategies to manage stress. Kaur and Murthy (1986) also reported that a significant difference in the coping strategies adopted by individuals working at different organizational levels. The reason may be that there was a positive and significant relationship between role stress and avoidance strategies, between roles stress and externality, and between externality and avoidance strategies. Organizational role stress was negatively and significantly associated with approach strategies.

The finding of the study revealed that majority of the respondents console themselves with the hope that things will get better. Similar finding was reported by Verma et al. (1995) that among the college students, the females resorted to prayer and hoped for the better. Females became more emotionally upset as compared to males who confronted the problem and made an attempt to solve it.

The finding of the study also revealed that majority of the respondents maintained good relationship with others especially those closer to them. Similar finding was also reported by Christopher (2001) that on role satisfaction and role conflict among married working women, majority of married working women, have expressed satisfaction in their role performance at work in the aras like duration of work, professional fulfillment, equal status and good relationship with the superiors.

## SUGGESTIONS TO REDUCE THE PROBLEMS OF WORKING WOMEN

The findings of the study revealed that the majority of the respondents opined that to stop women's harassment at workplace, the Law should be strongly implemented by the organization, Separate toilet facility for women should be compulsory. Further, the working women also suggested that to increase positive attitude towards working women, the awareness about equality of women should be increased in the society and in each organization.

The fact cannot be denied that while performing dual roles, women had to face job related problems and household work related problems. Thus, it becomes highly important for the working women especially for the married working women, to fulfill their role requirements adequately and satisfactorily when they play such multiple roles. On the other side, this in turn, leads to role conflicts, which affects both their familial, work environment and relations. This often makes women more tense producing a high degree of stress on them. They perform family responsibilities and job at the expense of their physical and psychological health. Therefore, in this context, the need for professional counseling may emerge and may be felt by the working women its need and scope in order to help them to overcome their problems and conflicts smoothly and positively. The society has to create a parallel infrastructure to reduce the drudgery of the multiple roles of working women. Social barriers can be broken if the families accept their supportive role in the changing life style of the women.

Thus, along with the family, the organization sectors could also play a constructive role in reducing the problems of working women. The workplace needs to provide facilities like transportation, separate toilets, vocational training to increase efficiency along with the congenial atmosphere at workplace.

# 6

# SUMMARY AND CONCLUSION

## INTRODUCTION

A woman is the mother of the race and liaison between generations. It is the mother who have sustained the growth of the society and moulded the future of the nation. In the emerging complex social scenario, women have a pivotal role to play. They can no longer be considered as mere harbingers of peace, but they are emerging as a source of power and a symbol of progress. In Indian society, she has played and continuous role. Variation in the status of woman according to the cultural milieu, family structure, case, class and proprietary rights etc. have been taking place from time to time. Her role in various walks of life has greatly contributed to the evolution of values, which lead to all round progress of society at large.

Since the times immemorial, worth of the work done or services rendered by women has not been recognized. India is a multifaceted society where no generalization could apply to the entire nation's various regional, religious, social, and economic groups. Working women do use and spend their income at their own will but sometimes permission of the husband becomes necessary for the purpose. After globalization women are able to get more jobs but the work they get is more casual in nature or is the one that men do not prefer to do or is left by them to move to higher or better jobs.

Most of the women work to help their families in their economic disparities. The women in general suffer from some of the assumptions and prejudices which the authorities particularly the male, have towards them. The management feels that women are not serious or efficient workers. They put in less work and come only to pass time. As soon as they get married, they will go away. Maternity, childcare, transfer of husbands, work demands of the husband and family will make them give up jobs, play truant or become indifferent and efficient.

In the modern world, the women have to perform two challenging roles- one of the housewife and mother of a wage earner for supplementing the family income so that standard of living and quality of life of her family can be enhanced. In discharging her dual role at home and workplace and to strike an optimal balance amongst them, her satisfaction level varies.

The crux of the problem of women's employment lies in the dilemma of her dual responsibilities in being a housewife, a mother as well as an employee and a producer of income for her family. Women are gradually realizing that they have personalities of their own as human beings. Their mission in life does not end with becoming good wives and wise mothers only, but also realizing that they are all equal members. Being a member of the family, each individual has a specific expectation from a woman. The in-laws have expectations from the daughter-in-law, the husband from the wives, and the children from their mother.

Working women's problems are aggravated by their multiple role expectations which we find in Indian society. A woman taking up a job outside, home also has to look after domestic work along with her official work. This dual responsibility has overburdened working women, thereby leading to multidimensional problems. Working women have a much larger area of social interaction. They get opportunity to meet more varied kinds of people. They have their own circle of colleagues.

Consistent with the long-term trend the presence of women in work force continues to increase. The employment of women has opened up new vistas for women; shifting interest from household duties to work outside. Women work double the time than their counterparts. Attending to the daily household chores, looking after the children, family members and also working a full day in paid employment, she has no time to relax. Women employees face the problem of transfer in job placement as per ordered by the job authority, which becomes a critical situation for them, as they cannot get rid of family responsibilities. The participation of women in employment outside home has greatly changed their family lives.

Since primary responsibilities of the women revolve with home and children, so despite the arrangement made to ease their burden, they require to work at home in addition to their outdoor duties. Constant attention of the mother and her physical presence are considered important to provide healthy psychological environment for the development of a child's personality. Carrying out almost single handedly all the duties and responsibilities of family, overstrain a working women and makes her tired and irritable, which in turn is liable to make her unpleasant and unenjoyable company to her husband, children and their family members.

## OBJECTIVES OF THE STUDY

1. To study the *problems faced by working women* in the city of Baroda.
2. To study the problems of working women *in relation to* their-
   (a) Job related problems
   (b) Household work related problems
3. To study the differences *in the overall problems* of working women with respect to the following variables.
   - Age
   - Experience
   - Type of family
   - Distance from workplace
4. To study the differences in the *Job related problems* of working women with respect to the following variables:
   - Age
   - Experience
   - Type of family
   - Distance from workplace

5. To study the differences in the *Household work related problems* of working women with respect to the following variables:
   - Age
   - Experience
   - Type of family
   - Distance from workplace
6. To study the *coping up strategies* used by the working women to manage stress.
7. To obtain the *suggestions* to reduce the problems of working women.

## ASSUMPTION OF THE STUDY

1. Working women use coping up strategies to manage stress due to their multiple roles.

## NULL HYPOTHESES OF THE STUDY

1. There will be no significant differences *in the overall problems of* working women with respect to the following variables:
   - Age
   - Experience
   - Type of family
   - Distance from workplace
2. There will be no significant differences in the *Job related problems* of working women with respect to the following variables:
   - Age
   - Experience
   - Type of family
   - Distance from workplace
3. There will be no significant differences in the *Household work related problems* of working women with respect to the following variables:
   - Age
   - Experience
   - Type of family
   - Distance from workplace

## METHODOLOGY

### *DESCRIPTION OF POPULATION*

To study the problems of working women of Baroda city of Gujarat State were selected. Hence the working women in the year 2008-09 were taken as population of the study.

## *SELECTION OF SAMPLES AND SAMPLING METHOD*

The sample of the present study consisted of 120 working women from Baroda. The Purposive Sampling method was used to select the sample of the study.

## *CONSTRUCTION OF RESEARCH TOOL*

The Structured Questionnaire for collecting the information for the study of Problems of working women of Baroda in the year 2008-09 was constructed from various books, journals, and papers, personal experience of the investigation and also through discussion with experts. The various sections of the questionnaire were developed according to the objectives. The Questionnaire was in English as well as in Gujarati language.

## *VALIDITY OF THE TOOL*

The Questionnaire was given to experts for checking the appropriateness of the tool for its content, response system and the language used. The experts had suggested certain minor changes in the questionnaire which were incorporated before pretesting the questionnaire.

## *PRETESTING OF THE RESEARCH TOOL*

Pre-Testing of the tool was done to check the clarity of the language and to find out the time required by the respondents to fill up the Questionnaire. The translated questionnaires were distributed to ten working women of different professions during the month of October-November 2008 which was excluded from the final data. The data collected for pre-testing were analyzed and some changes in the Questionnaire were made.

## *COLLECTION OF DATA*

The data was collected in the month of November- December 2008. The investigator had personally distributed the Questionnaires and collected Data.

## SCORING AND CATEGORIZATION

*Scoring and Categorization of the Independent and Dependent Variables:* The variables which were not categorized in the questionnaire were clustered into categories to test the hypotheses.

**Categorization of the Independent Variables**

| *Variables* | *Basis* | *Category* |
|---|---|---|
| Age | 20-29 Yrs· | Young |
| | 30-39 Yrs· | Middle |
| | 40 Yrs and Above | Old |
| Type of family | — | Joint |
| | | Nuclear |
| | | Extended |
| Experience | 1-6 Yrs | Novice |
| | 7-12 Yrs | Less |
| | 13 Yrs and Above | More |
| Distance from workplace | Upto 2 kms | Near |
| | 3 kms to 6 kms· | Fairly Distant |
| | 7 kms or more | Distant |

**Categorization of the Dependent Variables**

| *Variables* | *Basis* | *Category* |
|---|---|---|
| Educational Qualification | Post Graduate and Post Graduate Diploma Holder | Post Graduate |
| | Graduate and Diploma Holder | Graduate |
| | HSC Pass and below 12th Pass | Under Graduate |
| Family size | 1-3 members· | Small |
| | 4-6 members· | Medium |
| | 7 members or more | Large |
| Monthly income of the respondent | Upto Rs. 10,000 | Low |
| | Rs. 10,000 or more | More |
| Number of earning members | Upto 2 members | Few |
| | 3 or more members | Many |
| Family Income | Below Rs. 19,000 | Average |
| | Above Rs. 19,000 | More than average |
| Job Designation | Engineer, Advocate, Administrative officer, Supervisor, Accountant, Financial Accountant | Class I |
| | College Teacher, School Teacher, NGO Worker, Clerks, Nurses, Telesales Executives, Micro Biologist | Class II |

*Contd.*

| | | |
|---|---|---|
| | Attendant, Data Preparation Assistant, Accountant Assistant, Private Secretary | Class III |
| Working hours | 3-5 hours | Less than normal |
| | 6-8 hours | Normal |
| | More than 8 hours | More than normal |
| Mode of Transport | — | Personal Conveyance provided by Office· Public Transport· By walking |

## MAJOR FINDINGS OF THE STUDY

1. Majority of the Respondents were from younger age group, belonged to nuclear family and Hindu Religion.
2. Majority of the Respondent were working from 1-6 years and were staying atleast upto 2 kms Distance from their workplace.
3. Majority of the Respondents were Graduate; little more than thirty percent of the Respondents were Post Graduate whereas less than fifteen percent of the Respondents were Under Graduate also.
4. High majority of the Respondents had Own or Self Possessed house.
5. Majority of the Respondents had 4-6 members in their family and were married, and had upto 2 earning members in their family.
6. High majority of the Respondents had 1-2 children and got sufficient time to do household activities.
7. Majority of the Respondents were earning above Rs. 19,000 family income per month and belonged to class III as their job Designation.
8. High majority of the Respondents were satisfied with their present job, having independent office, found their workplaces comfortable enough to meet their job demands.

9. The intensity indices on Job related problems of working women items like, No transportation services; No rest room facility; No canteen facility available in the organization; do not get promotion in the job and Get tired due to work were the problems which the respondents faced more at their workplaces.
10. The intensity indices on Household work related problems like, Unable to help husband for such activities like go to pay Telephone and Mobile bills, Electricity bills, different Taxes etc; Unable to fulfill hobbies like knitting, reading, painting etc. due to lack of time; unable to give full attention to the needs of my children; Unable to attend relatives/ guests at home and Unable to attend social functions like marriage ceremonies and other functions were the problems which the respondents faced more in their Household work.
11. The intensity indices on Coping up Strategies used by working women to manage stress like, Maintain good relationships with others, Try and enjoy moments of pleasure; Organize the time to do things that are important to women; Take situations as an opportunity to learn; Console with the hope that things will get better; Try to control the situation around them; Practice meditation and Can make decisions without undue anxiety were the coping up strategies strongly agreed and agreed by the respondents.
12. Problems of working women in relation to variables

| *Variables* | *Overall* | *Job Related* | *Household Work Related* |
|---|---|---|---|
| Age | Sig* | N.S. | Sig* |
| Type of family | N.S. | N.S. | N.S. |
| Experience | N.S. | N.S. | Sig* |
| Distance from workplace | N.S. | N.S. | N.S. |

* Sig at 0.05 level

13. There were *significant differences* in the overall problems of working women in relation to their *Age* and *no significant differences* in the overall problems of working women in relation to their *Type of family*, *Experience* and *Distance from the workplace.*

14. There were *no significant differences* in the job related problems of working women in relation to their *Age, Type of family, Experience* and *Distance from the workplace.*
15. There were *Significant differences* in the household work related problems of working women in relation to their *Age* and *Experience* and there were *no significant differences* in the household related problems of working women related to their Household work in relation to their *Type of family* and *Distance from workplace.*
16. High majority of the respondents had agreed to a great extent for following suggestions to reduce the problems of working women:
    - Separate toilet facility for women should be compulsory.
    - The rule should be strongly implemented to stop women's harassment at workplace by the organization.
    - The awareness should be increased in the society to increase positive attitude towards working women.
    - There is a need to change/ mould the attitude of the male-members of our families.
    - Team work, unity and love should be both at home and workplace so that one feels cheerful to work without any stress and complaints.
    - In work place, if a man and a woman are at same position, both of them should be given equal importance when it comes to decision making.
    - Timing should be made flexible keeping in mind women's convenience.

## CONCLUSION

The present study is an attempt to find out the Job related problems and Household work related problems of working women of Baroda. The women were overburdened with dual responsibilities of household work and job. Marriage and employment increase the roles and responsibilities of the women. It is difficult for the working women to fulfill their roles and requirements adequately and satisfactorily. In the job situation, good working conditions including the support from colleagues, superiors along with good intrapersonal relationships and opportunities for advancement could play a vital role in reducing the problems of working women. Thus, in the changing social cultural environment, women are entering into a new era, but they are still overburdened. So, some measures should be introduced to overcome their problems for the efficient management of their multiple roles.

Ironically, on the whole situation of working women was not totally satisfactory. Moreover, the working women have perceived their official and domestic dimensions of life satisfaction but there are irritants and obstacles to, which need to be resolved.

The working women face various problems and difficulties in job and family relations. While performing the dual responsibilities of job and household work, the women are not able to fulfill all the expectations of the family. If she does not carry out her role efficiency as a wife and a mother, apart of being accused, she suffers from guilt conscious and finds herself ton between home and work. Thus, working women are generally haunted by the feeling of guilt. As a result of such multiple role demands, she cannot possibly do justice to all these roles. The consequence of this is a cognitive state of 'role strain' which is the felt difficulty of fulfilling role obligations. Thus, the attitude of the husband and family members needs to be changed towards the working women. Moreover, husband should come forward to share her burden, thereby reducing the drudgery of the multiple roles of a working woman. Hence, family can create an environment of equal expectations by performing their supportive role in the changing life styles of the working women.

Apart from family, the psychological well being of women has considerable impact on her performance and productivity at her job. In the job, women need to be given adequate infrastructural facilities and opportunity for advancement, healthy interpersonal relationship in terms of adequate support and help at workplace.

Therefore, workplaces need to provide congenial atmosphere at job including the facilities like professional counseling and welfare services and organizing training programmes etc. so that women can overcome the psychological stress and can play their roles efficiently and effectively.

## RECOMMENDATIONS FOR FURTHER STUDIES

The investigator on the basis of her experience and findings of the study recommends studies in the following areas:

- A similar study can be conducted with women administrators from different professions and cadres other than those included in this study.
- A similar study can be carried out in relation to the other variables such as occupational adjustment, educational qualification and marital status.
- A study can be undertaken to find out the perceptions/attitudes of superiors and subordinates on the efficiency and capacities of the women employees.
- A comparative study can be undertaken on the job satisfactions of women employees.
- A multivariate study can be conducted on problems and concerns of employed women according to type of occupation and type of family structure.

# BIBLIOGRAPHY


Agarwal, K. (1988), Status and Role of Middle class Educated Earning Women in the Indian Family. In: Dak, T.M. Women and Work in Indian Society, Discovery Publishing House, New Delhi.

Agrwal, R. ( 2001), Stress in Life and Work. Sage Publications, New Delhi, January.

Anand, N. (2003), Working Women-Issues and Problems, *Yojana*, 47(3), March. pp. 11-14.

Arya, R. (1990), Women in Public Sectors. Madak Publications Pvt. Ltd., New Delhi.

Banerji, A. and Sen, R.K. (2000), Women and Economic Development. Deep and Deep Publications Pvt. Ltd., New Delhi.

Bhatia, J. (1988), Impact of Employment of Women from Low Socio-Economic Status in the Selected Colony of Delhi on their life in relation to the selected variables, Dissertation (M.Sc)............ Faculty of Home Science, The M.S. University of Baroda.

Bhoite (1988), A. Employed Women – A Sociological Perspective *In*: Dak, T.M. Women and Work in Indian Society. Discovery Publishing House, New Delhi.

Bradburn, N. (1969), The Structure of Well-being. Chicago: Aldine.

Christopher, A.J. (2001), Role Satisfaction and Role Conflicts among Married Working Women. *Social Welfare*. 48(5), August. pp. 15-24.

Coverman, E. (1985), Explaining Husband's Participation in Domestic Labour. *Sociological Quarterly* 26, pp. 81-97

Deshpande, L. (1992), Problems of Working Wives, A Study of Family Adjustment Pattern, Dissertation (M.SW).......Faculty of Social Work, The M.S. University of Baroda.

Devi, L.V. (1982), Status and Employment of Women in India; B.R. Publishing Corporation, Delhi.

Dubey, M. (1982), Working Women and their Problems. Dissertation (MSW)....Faculty of Social Work, M.S. University of Baroda.

Gore, M. (1988), Problems and Progress of Women in Management. National Publishing House, New Delhi.

Hazarika, D. (1991), Employed Women's Traditional and Modern Home Making Responsibilities in Association with their Physical Facilities, Attitudes, Problems and Inferences for Home Science Curriculum. Thesis (Ph.D.).........The M.S. University of Baroda

Hofferth, R. and Moore, H. (1978), Working Wives and Family. Mayfield Publishing Company, New York.

Kalia, H.L. (1999), Occupational Health Survey of Women in Industry. *Social Welfare,* 46(1) , April. pp. 6-11.

Kapoor, V. (1984) Stress and Coping Style of Educated Mother Gainfully Employed outside the Home. Master's Dissertation Baroda, The M.S. University of Baroda.

Kaur, G. and Murthy, V.N. (1986), Organizational Roles Stress, Coping Strategies and Locus of Control in a Major Public Sector Industrial Organization. Unpublished manuscript.

Kraisonswasdi, N. (1989), Women Executives- A Sociological Study in Role Effectiveness. Jaipur, Rawat Publications, pp. 53-65.

——(1990), Kyodo Report, Tokyo. March 21 p. 4

Lalitha, U. (1982), Stress and Employment of Women in India. B.R. Publishing House, New Delhi.

Lazarus, R.S. (1987), The Psychology of Coping: Issues of Research and Assessment. In G.V. Coelho, D.A. Hamburg and J.E. Adams (Eds.), Coping and adaptation. New York: Basic Books, 1974a.

Mani, G. (1987), Working Mothers in Madras City. *Journal of Social Welfare* Vol XXXIV No. 6 Sept. pp. 29-30.

Mathews, M. (1990), Psycho Social Study of Working Women. Dissertation (MSW).....Faculty of Social Work, The M.S. University of Baroda.

Mukhopadhyay, L. (1999), Stress in the Lives of Working Women and Coping Mechanisms. *Social Welfare,* 46(4), July. pp. 26-29.

Murty, S. (2001), Women and Employment. RBSA Publishers, Jaipur.

Pareek ((1983b), Preventing and Resolving Conflict. In L.D. Goodstein and J.W. Pfeiffer (Eds.), The 1983 Annual for Facilitators, Trainers and Consultants (164-169). San Diego, California: University Associates.

Parikh, J. and Shah, N. (1994), Women Managers in Transition-From Homes to Corporate Offices. Indian Journal of Social Work. Vol. 48(2), April.

Patel, U. (1988 ), Problems of Working Women in India. In: Dak, T.M. Women and Work in Indian Society. Discovery Publishing House, New Delhi, pp. 211-232

Pestonjee, D.M. (1999), Stress and Coping, The Indian Experience. Sage Publications, New Delhi.

Rath, S. (1987), Working Women in Cuttack. *Social Welfare.* Vol. XXXIV No. 1, April. pp. 4-6.

Rawat, P. (2004), A Study on the Problems of Working Women from the Selected Public Sectors, Baroda. Dissertation (M.Sc)..... Faculty of Home Science, The M.S. University of Baroda.

Reddy, C. (1986), Chaining Status of Educated Working Women, B.R. Publishing Corporation, New Delhi.

Renne, K.S. (1974), Measurement of Social Health in General Population Survey. Social Science Research, 3, 25-44.

Sinha, P.R. and Prabha, S. (1988), Status Equilibrium of Working Women. *In*: Dak, T.M. Women and Work in Indian Society. Discovery Publishing House, New Delhi.

Stead, A. (1985), Women in Management. New Jersey, Prentice Hall Pub. Inc., pp. 109-123.

Sundaram, K.K. (1984), Dhandapani, R.D. and Narayana-swamy, N. How do Women Cope up with Home and Job? *Journal of Social Welfare* Vol XXXI No. 2 May pp. 22-36.

Swarnalata (1986), Women IAS Officers on their Dual Roles. *Journal of Social Welfare.* Vol XXXII No. 12 March, pp. 13-14.

Verma, S., Duggal, S. and Supriya (1995), Effective Coping Strategies in College Students. *Journal of Psychological Researches,* 39 (1-2), 7-13.

# APPENDICES

*Appendix-I*

## QUESTIONNAIRE

*Direction: Please read the following items carefully and tick mark (√) the appropriate alphabet depicting your answer in the space provided.*

### SECTION I
### BACKGROUND INFORMATION

1. Age of the respondent:
   (a) 20-24 Years
   (b) 25-29 Years
   (c) 30-34 Years
   (d) 35-39 Years
   (e) 40-44 Years
   (f) 45 Years and Above
2. Religion of the respondent:
   (a) Hindu
   (b) Muslim
   (c) Shikh
   (d) Christian
   (e) Any other __________
3. Educational Qualification of the respondent:
   (a) Post Graduate and Above
   (i.e. M.A., M.Com., M.Sc., Ph.D etc.)
   (b) Post Graduate Diploma holder
   (i.e., Diploma after SSc or HSC)
   (c) Graduate
   (i.e., B.A., B.Com., B.Sc., B.E. etc.)
   (d) Diploma Holder
   (i.e., Diploma after Graduation)
   (e) HSC Pass
   (i.e., 12th Pass)
   (f) Below 12th Pass
   (g) Any other, please specify________

4. Residence of the respondent:
   (a) Own house (b) Rented house
   (c) Quarter provided by the employer
5. Type of Family:
   (a) Joint (b) Nuclear
   (c) Extended
6. How many members do you have in your family? (Including yourself)
   (a) 1(yourself) (b) 2
   (c) 3 (d) 4
   (e) 5 (g) 7 or more
   (f) 6
7. Marital Status of the respondent:
   (a) Single (b) Married
   (c) Widow (d) Separated
   If married, how many children do you have?
   (a) None (b) 1
   (c) 2 (d) 3 or more
8. Your monthly salary:
   (a) Below Rs. 5,000 (b) Rs. 5,001 to Rs. 10,000
   (c) Rs. 10,001 to Rs. 15,000 (d) Above Rs. 15,001
9. How many members of your family are earning?
   (a) 1 (b) 2
   (c) 3 (d) 4 or more
10. Family Income per Month:
    (a) below Rs. 9000 (b) Rs. 9001-Rs. 14,000
    (c) Rs. 14,001 – Rs. 19,000 (d) Rs. 19,001- Rs. 24,000
    (e) Rs. 24,001- Rs. 29,000 (f) Above Rs. 29,001
11. How does your family respond to your job?
    (a) Supportive (b) Co-operative
    (c) Helpful (d) Any other_______
12. Do you get sufficient time to do household activities?
    (a) Yes (b) No
    If Yes, then who helps you in household activities?

| *Activities* | *Self* | *Mother in Law* | *Other Members of the Family* | *House Maid* | *Any Other* |
|---|---|---|---|---|---|
| Cooking | | | | | |
| Cleaning | | | | | |
| Shopping | | | | | |
| Any other | | | | | |

13. Job Designation:
    (a) Engineer (b) Doctor
    (c) Magistrate (d) Advocate
    (e) Police (f) Administrative Officer
    (g) College Teacher (h) School Teacher
    (i) NGO Worker (j) Clerk
    (k) Nurse (l) Any other_______
14. At what age you started your job?
    (a) Below 25 years (b) 25 - 27 years
    (c) 28-30 years (d) 31-33 years
    (e) 34-36 years (f) above 36 years
15. Since how long you have been working?
    (a) 1-3 years (b) 4-6 years
    (c) 7-9 years (d) 10-12 years
    (e) 13-15 years (f) above 15 years
16. What are your working hours?
    (a) 3-5 hours (b) 6-8 hours
    (c) More than 8 hours
17. Are there specific times when you have to stay back at work for long hours?
    (a) Yes (b) No
18. Why did you join the job?
    (a) To supplement family income
    (b) To attain economic independence
    (c) To raise the standard of living of the family
    (d) To provide better education to children
    (e) To develop own personality
    (f) To keep oneself busy
    (g) To utilize one's education
    (h) Any other. Please Specify__________

19. Have you worked anywhere else before taking up the present job?
    (a) Yes (b) No
    If yes, what were the reasons for changing the earlier job?
    (a) Due to less salary
    (b) Due to poor work environment
    (c) The work place was far from the house
    (d) Unpleasant atmosphere at workplace
    (e) Transfer of father/ husband
    (f) Any other. Please specify_________
20. Why did you select this present job?
    (a) For better prospects in career
    (b) For better salary
    (c) For having interest in doing job
    (d) Workplace being near to the house
    (e) Any other. _______________
21. What are the sources of getting this job?
    (a) Campus Recruitment
    (b) Friends
    (c) Family members and Relatives
    (d) Employment Exchange
    (e) Advertisements
    (f) Any other _______________
22. What type of facilities/ benefits do you get from the Management?
    (a) Canteen (b) Separate toilets for women
    (c) Separate rest rooms (d) Maternity Care/ Leave
    (e) Creches (f) Medical Care
    (g) Any other. _____________
23. Are you satisfied with your present job?
    (a) Yes (b) No
    If Yes, give the reasons for satisfaction?
    (a) Because of getting good Salary
    (b) Because of good Work Environment

(c) Due to workplace nearer to the house
(d) Due to job as per choice
(e) Any other ____________

24. Do you have an independent office?
(a) Yes (b) No
If yes, then do you have adequate furniture available in your office?
(a) Yes (b) No

25. Specify category of your job:
(a) Skilled (b) Semi skilled
(c) Unskilled

26. What type of behavior do you get from your colleagues?
(a). Understanding (b) Supportive
(c) Courteous (d) Friendly
(e) Co-operative (f) Resentful
(g) Humiliating

27. Do you find your working place comfortable enough to meet your job demands?
(a) Yes (b) No

28. Does your job effects your status in society?
(a) Yes (b) No

29. What is the distance of your workplace from home?
(a) Less than 1 km (b) 1 – 2 kms
(c) 3 – 4 kms (d) 5 – 6 kms
(e) 7 – 8- kms (f) More than 8 kms

30. Which mode of transport do you use to reach office?
(a) City Bus
(b) Auto rickshaw
(c) Personal Conveyance
(d) Conveyance Provided by Office
(e) By walking
(f) Any Other

## SECTION II

*Following are some problems related to work and you are requested to identify. Kindly indicate your problems with a tick (") in the appropriate box.*

| *Problems* | *Yes* | *No* |
|---|---|---|
| **Job related problems:** | | |
| No transportation services are provided by the organization. | | |
| There is no separate toilet for women in organization. | | |
| No rest room facility is available in the organization. | | |
| There is no canteen facility available in the organization. | | |
| I have to work with the people whom I do not get along with. | | |
| I have to travel for work frequently. | | |
| have difficulty in staying alone in hotels while travelling alone for professional work. | | |
| I don't get peace of mind due to work. | | |
| My job demands extra hours of work. | | |
| I get tired due to work. | | |
| I am overloaded with the work which is greater than that of the other colleagues. | | |
| My pay is not adequate to fulfill my financial needs. | | |
| I do not get promotion in the job. | | |
| I do not get adequate powers to perform my job in a better manner. | | |
| I do not get fair treatment from my colleagues. | | |
| I am unable to concentrate on the work due to some of the peculiar habits of my co-workers like too much of interference in my work. | | |
| I do not get help from other colleagues. | | |
| My colleagues dominate me. | | |
| There is internal jealously among the staff members, which hamper the professional growth. | | |
| There is negative propaganda by male staff which is harming the professional status and personal life. | | |
| My superiors do not consider my personal genuine problems. | | |
| My authorities indicate favourism/bias towards other employees. | | |
| My job does not give me enough experiences, which leads to dissatisfaction. | | |
| I find lack of opportunity for advancement in the job attending training programmes. | | |

I do not get time to attend seminars/workshops/ lectures for professional growth.
My suggestions are not accepted by subordinates like in official matters or in organizing any official programmes.
I have sleep disturbances due to job stress.
I do not get appreciation for my work.
I usually fear that I might be terminated from the job.
I have to suffer due to my job place is far from my home.
I have recently shifted to new job, which is stressful.
I feel I am not given well deserved promotion.
I feel I get less salary as compared to people in organization of similar size.
I am not happy with the commute between work and home.
I feel that my life is usually filled with deadlines.
*Household work related problems:*
I have difficulty in carrying out family responsibilities like unable to cope up with the work at home.
I am overburdened at home like taking care of sick/ elderly family members.
I am unable to spend peaceful time with family members during holidays.
I am unable to work according to the expectation of my family members like going out for vacations, cooking their favourite meal etc.
I am unable to attend relatives/ guests at home.
I do not get cooperation from my family members in sharing household responsibilities.
I lack confidence in housekeeping tasks.
I do not find reliable servant which creates difficulty in managing household work.
My servant remains absent in the peak hours of work.
My servant is not efficient.
I cannot afford a servant.
I am unable to attend social functions like marriage ceremonies and other functions.
I have to fulfill too many social expectations/ obligations.
I do not get cooperation from my husband.
My husband is not satisfied with my household work.

I am neglected from my husband.
My in laws complaint to my husband regarding my household work.
I am unable to fulfill my hobbies like knitting, reading, painting etc. due to lack of time.
My children are too small and I cannot leave them alone.
There is non-availability of day care centers/ pre-nursery /play centers near home/workplace.
I am unable to give full attention to the needs of my children.
I am unable to help my children in doing their academic work.
My children perform below expectations due to lack of guidance by me.
My children suffer in studies as they have to do household work.
There is a lack of children's park nearby.
Conflicts take place between my husband and me pertaining to children.
Disputes take place between my family members and me pertaining to household duties.
I do not get any preferential treatment in the family on account of being working women like not giving consideration to my opinion in family decisions.
I face opposition of family members for my job.
I never handled any responsibility as I was over protected.
I have lack of time due to overburden of housekeeping activities.
I am unable to help my husband for such activities like go to pay Telephone and Mobile bills, Electricity bills , different Taxes etc.
I am unable to adjust myself with the changing life.
I have less interest in doing household activities.
I have to suffer due to expectations of family members for hot meal food.

**SECTION III**

*Following are the statements regarding Coping up Strategies of working women. Your agreement and disagreement will be determined largely in terms of your particular experience. Make a tick mark (√) at the appropriate response depicting your answer in the space provided.*

SA – If you strongly agree with the statement.
A – If you agree with the statement.
DA – If you disagree with the statement.
SD – If you strongly disagree with the statement.

| *Statements* | *SA* | *A* | *DA* | *SD* |
|---|---|---|---|---|
| *When I am under stress I try to cope with the situation using the following:* | | | | |
| I exercise. | | | | |
| I include regular breathing exercises. | | | | |
| I practice meditation. | | | | |
| I smoke. | | | | |
| I take more fried and heavy food. | | | | |
| I increase my caffeine intake (Coffee, Tea, and Cola). | | | | |
| I compulsively work. | | | | |
| I set myself unrealistic goals. | | | | |
| I blame other people. | | | | |
| I plan ahead for events that may be potentially stressful. | | | | |
| I organize my time to do things that are important to me. | | | | |
| I can make decisions without undue anxiety. | | | | |
| I try to help others. | | | | |
| I take enough breaks to reduce the monotonous nature of my work. | | | | |
| I try to control the situation around me. | | | | |
| I try to change situations. | | | | |
| I take situations as an opportunity to learn. | | | | |
| I try to change my priorities. | | | | |
| I compromise to get something positive out of the situation. | | | | |
| I console myself with the hope that things will get better. | | | | |
| I try to get out of the situation gracefully. | | | | |
| I physically withdraw myself from the situation. | | | | |
| I postpone decisions pertaining to the problem. | | | | |

I give the situation extra attention.
I often try to use humor to diffuse tension.
I include some relaxation time in my daily routine.
I try and enjoy moments of pleasure.
I maintain good relationships with others, especially those closest to me.
I have someone with whom I discuss personal worries or problems.
I express what I feel or believe without feeling anxious.
I deny that there is a problem.

**SECTION IV**

*Direction: Following are the statements regarding the suggestions to reduce the problems of working women. Please tick mark (√)-*

GE – if you agree with the statement to a great extent
LE – if you agree with the statement to a less extent
SE – if you agree with the statement to some extent

| *Suggestions* | *GE* | *SE* | *LE* |
|---|---|---|---|
| Canteen facility should be provided by the organization. | | | |
| Rest room facility should be provided by the organization for reducing tired during the recess time. | | | |
| In each organization, Separate toilet facility for women should be compulsory. | | | |
| Every sector should have a transportation service of its own. | | | |
| Strengthening of childcare facilities near the working place by the institutions. | | | |
| The entertaining programmes should be usually organized by the organization. | | | |
| Indoor games should be usually arranged by the organization. | | | |
| In house journals should be published regularly in the organization so that the women can present their own thoughts. | | | |
| Special functions should be organized in the organization like welcome to new employee, employee's leave or celebration of her birthday etc. | | | |

Women should be given vocational training to increase their efficiency.
Women should be trained to develop their capabilities of decision making.
Women should be made aware of their constitutional and legal rights by Educational Institutions.
Maternity benefit schemes should be enhanced by the Government.
The rule for providing enough salary to working women should be strongly implemented.
Women should be given substantial allowances for medical expenses.
To stop women's harassment at workplace, the rule should be strongly implemented by the organization.
More seminars, conferences and workshops should be organized for the working women.
Health services like health check-ups, yoga/ exercise should be organized time to time by the institution.
The organization should provide family welfare services and professional counseling services.
Working Women's Association should be formed.
Husband should come forward to share responsibilities.
Burden of household work of working women should be reduced.
To increase positive attitude towards working women, the awareness should be increased in the society.

Any other

______________________________________________

______________________________________________

______________________________________________

______________________________________________

______________________________________________

______________________________________________

______________________________________________

______________________________________________

______________________________________________

______________________________________________

## *Appendix-II*

## *Differences in the Problems of Eorking Women*

**Agewise Job Related Problems of Working Women**

*ANOVA*

| *Source of Variance* | | *Sum of Squares* | *df* | *Mean Square* | *F* | *Sig.* |
|---|---|---|---|---|---|---|
| I do not get adequate powers to perform my job in a better manner. | Between Groups | 1.464 | 2 | .732 | 3.609 | .030* |
| | Within Groups | 23.736 | 117 | .203 | | |
| | Total | 25.200 | 119 | | | |

*Significant at 0.05 level

**Type of family wise Job Related Problems of Working Women**

*ANOVA*

| *Source of Variance* | | *Sum of Squares* | *df* | *Mean Square* | *F* | *Sig.* |
|---|---|---|---|---|---|---|
| I feel I am not given well deserved promotion. | Between Groups | 1.574 | 2 | .787 | 4.039 | .020* |
| | Within Groups | 22.793 | 117 | .195 | | |
| | Total | 24.367 | 119 | | | |

*Significant at 0.05 level

**Experience wise Job Related Problems of Working Women**

*ANOVA*

| *Source of Variance* | | *Sum of Squares* | *df* | *Mean Square* | *F* | *Sig.* |
|---|---|---|---|---|---|---|
| My job does not give me enough experiences,which leads to dissatisfaction. | Between Groups | .914 | 2 | .457 | 3.545 | .032* |
| | Within Groups | 15.078 | 117 | .129 | | |
| | Total | 15.992 | 119 | | | |

*Significant at 0.05 level

**Distance wise Job Related Problems of Working Women**

*ANOVA*

| *Source of Variance* | | *Sum of Squares* | *df* | *Mean Square* | *F* | *Sig.* |
|---|---|---|---|---|---|---|
| No transportation services are provided by the organization. | Between Groups | 1.862 | 2 | .931 | 4.283 | .016* |
| | Within Groups | 25.438 | 117 | .217 | | |
| | Total | 27.300 | 119 | | | |
| There is no separate toilet for women in | Between Groups | 1.783 | 2 | .891 | 4.312 | .016* |
| | Within Groups | 24.184 | 117 | .207 | | |

*Contd.*

| *Source of Variance* | | *Sum of Squares* | *df* | *Mean Square* | *F* | *Sig.* |
|---|---|---|---|---|---|---|
| organization. | Total | 25.967 | 119 | | | |
| I do not get promotion in the job. | Between Groups | 1.471 | 2 | .735 | 3.172 | .046* |
| | Within Groups | 27.121 | 117 | .232 | | |
| | Total | 28.592 | 119 | | | |
| I have to suffer due to my job place is far from my home. | Between Groups | 2.666 | 2 | 1.333 | 8.543 | .000* |
| | Within Groups | 18.259 | 117 | .156 | | |
| | Total | 20.925 | 119 | | | |

*Significant at 0.05 level

**Age wise Household Related Problems of Working Women**

*ANOVA*

| *Source of Variance* | | *Sum of Squares* | *df* | *Mean Square* | *F* | *Sig.* |
|---|---|---|---|---|---|---|
| I do not get cooperation from my husband. | Between Groups | 11.591 | 2 | 5.795 | 26.477 | .000* |
| | Within Groups | 25.609 | 117 | .219 | | |
| | Total | 37.200 | 119 | | | |
| My husband is not satisfied with my household work. | Between Groups | 13.909 | 2 | 6.955 | 21.982 | .000* |
| | Within Groups | 37.016 | 117 | .316 | | |
| | Total | 50.925 | 119 | | | |
| I am neglected from my husband. | Between Groups | 9.395 | 2 | 4.698 | 22.369 | .000* |
| | Within Groups | 24.571 | 117 | .210 | | |
| | Total | 33.967 | 119 | | | |
| My in laws complaint my husband regarding my household work. | Between Groups | 11.102 | 2 | 5.551 | 20.068 | .000* |
| | Within Groups | 32.364 | 117 | .277 | | |
| | Total | 43.467 | 119 | | | |
| My children are too small and I cannot leave them alone. | Between Groups | 20.200 | 2 | 10.100 | 33.764 | .000* |
| | Within Groups | 35.000 | 117 | .299 | | |
| | Total | 55.200 | 119 | | | |
| There is non-availability of day care centres/pre-nursery/play centres near home/workplace. | Between Groups | 20.519 | 2 | 10.260 | 37.692 | .000* |
| | Within Groups | 31.847 | 117 | .272 | | |
| | Total | 52.367 | 119 | | | |
| I am unable to give full attention to the needs of my children. | Between Groups | 27.533 | 2 | 13.767 | 35.296 | .000* |
| | Within Groups | 45.634 | 117 | .390 | | |
| | Total | 73.167 | 119 | | | |
| I am unable to help my children in doing their academic work. | Between Groups | 22.743 | 2 | 11.371 | 32.805 | .000* |
| | Within Groups | 40.557 | 117 | .347 | | |
| | Total | 63.300 | 119 | | | |
| My children perform | Between Groups | 21.210 | 2 | 10.605 | 35.069 | .000* |

*Contd.*

| *Source of Variance* | | *Sum of Squares* | *df* | *Mean Square* | *F* | *Sig.* |
|---|---|---|---|---|---|---|
| below expectations due to lack of guidance by me. | Within Groups | 35.382 | 117 | .302 | | |
| | Total | 56.592 | 119 | | | |
| My children suffer in studies as they have to do household work. | Between Groups | 19.022 | 2 | 9.511 | 42.850 | .000* |
| | Within Groups | 25.970 | 117 | .222 | | |
| | Total | 44.992 | 119 | | | |
| There is lack of children's park nearby. | Between Groups | 19.566 | 2 | 9.783 | 42.497 | .000* |
| | Within Groups | 26.934 | 117 | .230 | | |
| | Total | 46.500 | 119 | | | |
| Conflicts take place between my husband and me pertaining to children. | Between Groups | 18.533 | 2 | 9.266 | 31.035 | .000* |
| | Within Groups | 34.934 | 117 | .299 | | |
| | Total | 53.467 | 119 | | | |
| I am unable to help my husband for such activities like go to pay Telephone and Mobile Bills, Electricity Bills, Different Taxes etc. | Between Groups | 25.351 | 2 | 12.675 | 24.466 | .000* |
| | Within Groups | 60.616 | 117 | .518 | | |
| | Total | 85.967 | 119 | | | |
| I have less interest in doing household activities. | Between Groups | 1.105 | 2 | .553 | 4.343 | .015* |
| | Within Groups | 14.887 | 117 | .127 | | |
| | Total | 15.992 | 119 | | | |
| I have to suffer due to expectations of family members for hot meal food. | Between Groups | 1.674 | 2 | .837 | 3.739 | .027* |
| | Within Groups | 26.193 | 117 | .224 | | |
| | Total | 27.867 | 119 | | | |

*Significant at 0.05 level

**Type of Family wise Differences in the Household Related Problems of Working Women**

*ANOVA*

| *Source of Variance* | | *Sum of Squares* | *df* | *Mean Square* | *F* | *Sig.* |
|---|---|---|---|---|---|---|
| I cannot afford a servant. | Between Groups | .518 | 2 | .259 | 3.885 | .023* |
| | Within Groups | 7.807 | 117 | .067 | | |
| | Total | 8.325 | 119 | | | |
| My children perform below expectations due to lack of guidance by me. | Between Groups | 2.856 | 2 | 1.428 | 3.110 | .048* |
| | Within Groups | 53.735 | 117 | .459 | | |
| | Total | 56.592 | 119 | | | |

*Significant at 0.05 level

**Experience wise Differences in the Household Related Problems of Working Women**

*ANOVA*

| *Source of Variance* | | *Sum of Squares* | *df* | *Mean Square* | *F* | *Sig.* |
|---|---|---|---|---|---|---|
| I do not get cooperation from my husband. | Between Groups | 9.004 | 2 | 4.502 | 18.680 | .000* |
| | Within Groups | 28.196 | 117 | .241 | | |
| | Total | 37.200 | 119 | | | |
| My husband is not satisfied with my household work. | Between Groups | 5.038 | 2 | 2.519 | 6.423 | .002* |
| | Within Groups | 45.887 | 117 | .392 | | |
| | Total | 50.925 | 119 | | | |
| I am neglected from my husband. | Between Groups | 6.051 | 2 | 3.026 | 12.681 | .000* |
| | Within Groups | 27.915 | 117 | .239 | | |
| | Total | 33.967 | 119 | | | |
| My in laws complaint my husband regarding my household work. | Between Groups | 4.405 | 2 | 2.202 | 6.597 | .002* |
| | Within Groups | 39.062 | 117 | .334 | | |
| | Total | 43.467 | 119 | | | |
| My children are too small and I cannot leave them alone. | Between Groups | 9.196 | 2 | 4.598 | 11.694 | .000* |
| | Within Groups | 46.004 | 117 | .393 | | |
| | Total | 55.200 | 119 | | | |
| There is non-availability of day care centres/pre-nursery/ play centres near home /workplace. | Between Groups | 10.622 | 2 | 5.311 | 14.885 | .000* |
| | Within Groups | 41.745 | 117 | .357 | | |
| | Total | 52.367 | 119 | | | |
| I am unable to give full attention to the needs of my children. | Between Groups | 13.929 | 2 | 6.965 | 13.756 | .000* |
| | Within Groups | 59.238 | 117 | .506 | | |
| | Total | 73.167 | 119 | | | |
| I am unable to help my children in doing their academic work. | Between Groups | 11.672 | 2 | 5.836 | 13.226 | .000* |
| | Within Groups | 51.628 | 117 | .441 | | |
| | Total | 63.300 | 119 | | | |
| My children perform below expectations due to lack of guidance by me. | Between Groups | 12.273 | 2 | 6.137 | 16.201 | .000* |
| | Within Groups | 44.318 | 117 | .379 | | |
| | Total | 56.592 | 119 | | | |
| My children suffer in studies as they have to do household work. | Between Groups | 9.629 | 2 | 4.815 | 15.930 | .000* |
| | Within Groups | 35.362 | 117 | .302 | | |
| | Total | 44.992 | 119 | | | |
| There is lack of children's park nearby. | Between Groups | 10.474 | 2 | 5.237 | 17.007 | .000* |
| | Within Groups | 36.026 | 117 | .308 | | |
| | Total | 46.500 | 119 | | | |
| Conflicts take place between my husband and me pertaining to children. | Between Groups | 10.223 | 2 | 5.111 | 13.830 | .000* |
| | Within Groups | 43.244 | 117 | .370 | | |
| | Total | 53.467 | 119 | | | |
| I do not get any preferential treatment | Between Groups | .657 | 2 | .329 | 3.084 | .050* |
| | Within Groups | 12.468 | 117 | .107 | | |

*Contd.*

| *Source of Variance* | | *Sum of Squares* | *df* | *Mean Square* | *F* | *Sig.* |
|---|---|---|---|---|---|---|
| in the family on account of being working woman like not giving consideration to my opinion in family decisions. | Total | 13.125 | 119 | | | |
| I am unable to help my husband for such activities like go to pay Telephone and Mobile Bills, Electricity Bills, Different Taxes etc. | Between Groups | 18.028 | 2 | 9.014 | 15.524 | .000* |
| | Within Groups | 67.938 | 117 | .581 | | |
| | Total | 85.967 | 119 | | | |
| I have less interest in doing household activities. | Between Groups | .914 | 2 | .457 | 3.545 | .032* |
| | Within Groups | 15.078 | 117 | .129 | | |
| | Total | 15.992 | 119 | | | |

*Significant at 0.05 level

**Distance wise Differences in the Household Related Problems of Working Women**

*ANOVA*

| *Source of Variance* | | *Sum of Squares* | *df* | *Mean Square* | *F* | *Sig.* |
|---|---|---|---|---|---|---|
| I do not get cooperation from my husband. | Between Groups | 1.854 | 2 | .927 | 3.069 | .050* |
| | Within Groups | 35.346 | 117 | .302 | | |
| | Total | 37.200 | 119 | | | |
| I am neglected from my husband. | Between Groups | 2.425 | 2 | 1.213 | 4.499 | .013* |
| | Within Groups | 31.541 | 117 | .270 | | |
| | Total | 33.967 | 119 | | | |
| My in laws complaint my husband regarding my household work. | Between Groups | 2.978 | 2 | 1.489 | 4.303 | .016* |
| | Within Groups | 40.489 | 117 | .346 | | |
| | Total | 43.467 | 119 | | | |
| My children are too small and I cannot leave them alone. | Between Groups | 3.228 | 2 | 1.614 | 3.634 | .029* |
| | Within Groups | 51.972 | 117 | .444 | | |
| | Total | 55.200 | 119 | | | |
| There is non-availability of day care centres/pre-nursery/play centres near home/workplace. | Between Groups | 3.254 | 2 | 1.627 | 3.876 | .023* |
| | Within Groups | 49.113 | 117 | .420 | | |
| | Total | 52.367 | 119 | | | |
| I am unable to give full attention to the needs of my children. | Between Groups | 4.135 | 2 | 2.067 | 3.504 | .033* |
| | Within Groups | 69.032 | 117 | .590 | | |
| | Total | 73.167 | 119 | | | |
| I am unable to help | Between Groups | 4.527 | 2 | 2.263 | 4.506 | .013* |

*Contd.*

| *Source of Variance* | | *Sum of Squares* | *df* | *Mean Square* | *F* | *Sig.* |
|---|---|---|---|---|---|---|
| my children in doing their academic work. | Within Groups | 58.773 | 117 | .502 | | |
| | Total | 63.300 | 119 | | | |
| There is lack of children's park nearby. | Between Groups | 3.055 | 2 | 1.527 | 4.113 | .019* |
| | Within Groups | 43.445 | 117 | .371 | | |
| | Total | 46.500 | 119 | | | |
| Conflicts take place between my husband and me pertaining to children. | Between Groups | 3.355 | 2 | 1.677 | 3.916 | .023* |
| | Within Groups | 50.112 | 117 | .428 | | |
| | Total | 53.467 | 119 | | | |

*Significant at 0.05 level

# INDEX